BEAR TALES

from the Canadian Rockies

See next page

Drawn & Etched by Thomas Landseer. 1823

Christmas 1998

BEAR TALES

from the Canadian Rockies

James:

Once you have read this book, henceforth you will be our designated grizzly Bear Expert. Terence

compiled & edited by

Brian Patton

FIFTH
HOUSE
PUBLISHERS

Front cover painting, *A Surprise Meeting*, Carl Rungius, Glenbow Collection, Calgary, Canada. Front plate drawing and etching, *Ursus Ferox* from *Fauna-Boreali-Americana* (London: John Murray, 1829).
Cover and interior design by Jeremy Drought / Last Impression Publishing Service.
Editor's Note: In general, the excerpts in this book have been reprinted as they appeared in their original form.

The publisher gratefully acknowledges the support of the Department of Canadian Heritage and The Canada Council for the Arts for our publishing program.

THE CANADA COUNCIL | LE CONSEIL DES ARTS
FOR THE ARTS | DU CANADA
SINCE 1957 | DEPUIS 1957

We acknowledge the finacial support of the Government of Canada through the Book Publishing Industry Development Program for our publishing activities.

Printed in Canada.

98 99 00 01 02 / 5 4 3 2 1

CANADIAN CATALOGUING IN PUBLICATION DATA

Main entry under title:

Bear tales from the Canadian Rockies

ISBN 1-894004-13-2 *

1. Bears—Rocky Mountains, Canadian (B.C. and Alta.)—Anecdotes.* 2. Bears—Rocky Mountains, Canadian (B.C. and Alta.)—Folklore.* 3. Rocky Mountains, Canadian (B.C. and Alta.) History.* I. Patton, Brian, 1943–

QL795.B4B42 1998   599.78'09711   C98-910352-8

Fifth House Ltd.
#9 – 6125, 11th Street SE
Calgary, Alberta, Canada T2H 2L6
1•800•360•8826

CONTENTS

ACKNOWLEDGEMENTS

*W*HEN my old friend Hälle Flygare initially suggested I do a book of bear stories from the Canadian Rockies, I had some misgivings. Weren't there already more than enough books about bears? However, with his encouragement, and that of Fifth House Publishers, I soon realized how this book might showcase many exciting and colourful stories, which are not only entertaining, but also an important part of the region's history and folklore. I thank Hälle for the suggestion and his subsequent encouragement.

While a few stories in this anthology were excerpted from books currently available, most were discovered in the collections of regional libraries and archives. Special thanks are due to Lena Goon, Mary Andrews, and Ted Hart of the Whyte Museum of the Canadian Rockies in Banff, and Glenda Cornforth of the Jasper-Yellowhead Museum in Jasper. The Glenbow Museum's Library and Archives and the University of Calgary's MacKimmie Library were also valuable resources.

Charlene Dobmeier guided this project from start to finish. Her opinions regarding my selections were invaluable, as were her editorial suggestions on chapter arrangement, titles, and introductory text.

Mike Kerr was a sounding board for ideas on book design and story selection throughout the project.

I owe a special thanks to Rick Kunelius for submitting an original piece for this anthology on short notice. It is the only selection written specifically for this book.

And finally, Rhonda Allen has shared her advice, support, and love throughout the project, even though she fears mosquitoes far more than bears.

Brian Patton
Canmore, Alberta
March 1998

About the Author

*B*RIAN PATTON was charged by a grizzly bear on his first ever backpacking trip in the Rockies. Fortunately, he didn't take it personally and, for the past thirty-five years, he has lived in the Rockies and developed a less confrontational relationship with bears. During this time, he has worked as a park ranger, naturalist, writer, and regional historian and has maintained a fascination with bears and bear stories.

Several of Brian's personal encounters with bears occurred while he was compiling *The Canadian Rockies Trail Guide*—the first comprehensive guide to the region's trails and a perennial bestseller since 1971. He is also the author of *Parkways of the Canadian Rockies* and editor of the popular anthology *Tales from the Canadian Rockies*. He currently lives in Canmore, where he provides research support and personal programming on the Canadian Rockies through his Mountain Research consulting firm.

Bruno Engler

Brian Patton

INTRODUCTION
Living with Bears

From the very beginning, men have sat around their fires telling and retelling stories of adventures with bears.

— Andy Russell, *Great Bear Adventures* —

*A*few years back, I worked as a naturalist in the north end of Banff Park. One of my evening programs was a campfire talk about bears. More specifically, I told bear stories, my own and those I'd heard, to illustrate the nature of black and grizzly bears in the Canadian Rockies. I soon discovered that once you start telling bear stories, neither rain, snow, mosquitoes, nor gathering darkness will discourage an audience from wanting to hear more.

Having lived and worked in bear country since I was a teenager, I have heard my share of bear stories and told more than my share. There is a fascination with bears that defies reason. People love them, fear them, and love to fear them. And once you start swapping bear tales around the campfire, you know you are in for a long evening.

In compiling this book, I reflected on the role bears have played in my life—the dozens of bears, black and grizzly, I've encountered in the backcountry, and the scores I've observed from the roadside, in campgrounds and even, in the bad old days, at the garbage dumps. At every stage of my life, even before I lived in the Rocky Mountains, there were bears.

One of my earliest childhood memories is of a bear encounter my parents and I had on a camping trip. A black bear invaded our campsite in the middle of the night and began poking around our picnic table. My mother heard it and woke my father.

"There's a bear outside! Grab Brian and get to the car!"

My parents scrambled from the tent on hands-and-knees, my father reached back and pulled me out of the tent, and then they ran through the woods. My mother reached the car first, then looked around to see where my father was.

"My God, you've got him by the feet," she cried.

Since I was still half asleep, my memory of the incident is somewhat vague—only a sense of danger and excitement followed by a quick trip through the darkened forest hanging upside down. It is one of my mother's favourite bear stories.

There were many more black bear encounters on summer holidays while I was growing up. Most of these bears were campground bears and roadside beggars, which were normally quite skittish and easily frightened. With the bravado of youth, I believed I could stand up to any bear.

Then, when I was eighteen years old, I came to work in the Rocky Mountains, where I learned about the other bear—one that didn't operate quite the same as your run-of-the-mill, campground black bear.

On my first-ever backpacking trip that summer, a companion and I were charged by a grizzly bear. The bear burst from the forest, hit the trail ahead at full gallop, and headed straight for us. As I stood facing the charging bear, there was only time for my partner, cowering behind me, to ask "What should we do?" and for me to answer "Don't move!" This was not an act of cool calculation based on an understanding of bears; I was simply frozen in my tracks by shock and fear. The bear broke off its charge less than ten metres in front of us, then went crashing into the bush below the trail. To this day, more than thirty-five years later, that grizzly's face, open-mouthed and beady-eyed, is imprinted in my memory as clearly as a photograph.

A week or so later, another friend and I were climbing a mountain when we spotted a large sow grizzly with two cubs in the scattered trees ahead. The bears hadn't seen us, so my partner decided we should yell and wave our arms to let them know we were there. Bad decision. The mother bear roared down the mountainside, halving the distance between us in a few seconds, and then reared up on her hind legs. She stood there, swinging her head from side-to-side and sniffing the air, and we could only await her decision—either to retreat or to dispose of these intruders. Luckily for us, she returned to her cubs and disappeared into the forest.

Since those early encounters, I have had numerous adventures with bears. I've also spent many hours simply observing them from a safe distance. I've watched a young grizzly playing in a meadow, splashing through meltwater pools and somersaulting across snowbanks like a child; a large grizzly passing rapidly across a wasteland of glacial moraine in the dying light of day, bound with great purpose toward an incredible, night-time ascent of a heavily crevassed, seven kilometre-long glacier; another grizzly jealously guarding a moose kill, hour-after-hour for several days, like an unrepentant miser, and madly charging after even the smallest bird that might try to steal a morsel.

Not all observation is voyeuristic. Occasionally there are philosophical moments when man and bear regard each other with simple curiosity. I was living at the ranger station beneath Mount Robson a few summers ago when, finding it difficult to sleep, I got up and went to sit on the front porch of my cabin. The first faint light of morning reflected off grey clouds, providing just enough illumination to reveal a small black bear making his way through the forest. When he reached a point opposite my porch, he noticed me sitting quietly in my chair. Head protruding from the bushes, he peered at me for the longest time, as if to say "What are you doing up at this hour?" I stared back, meeting his gaze. "Just you and me, bear. *Quo vadis?*"

In these moments, it is difficult to deny the intelligence of bears. We see ourselves reflected in their eyes, perhaps as we would appear in a wild world. I believe this is the root fascination we all have with bears— a recognition of another intelligence out there, trying to eke out a living in the wilderness. In the words of Andy Russell: "I gradually understood that being there was one thing, but to crawl mentally inside an animal and to think like it was another."

My own fascination with bears and their interaction with humans led to the creation of this book. Bear stories are a great oral tradition in the Canadian Rockies—an important part of the folklore of the region. The establishment of national parks in the Rockies, shortly after the completion of the Canadian Pacific Railway, brought a wide variety of people into contact with bears and resulted in a greater diversity of stories than from any other region in Canada. But the lore of the bear goes back much further than the arrival of the CPR. As long as there have been people in the Rocky Mountains, there have been bear stories to tell.

The first peoples who migrated southward along the range from the Siberian-Alaskan land bridge 11,000 years ago were in constant contact with both black and grizzly bears, present in much greater numbers than we see today. Experience and observation were disseminated by storytelling and transformed through imagination into myth.

There was no one to record the importance of bears to prehistoric North American cultures, but it likely resembled what was discovered in Native groups by the first European explorers.

Peigan, Kootenay, Shuswap, and Sekani were the principal resident tribes on the eastern and western slopes of the Rockies when the first fur traders arrived around 1800. Though none of these tribes imparted great spiritual significance to the black bear, they all held the grizzly in high esteem. The exalted position of grizzly bears was understandable. Size, power, and unpredictability made them the most dangerous animal in the Indians' world. To kill a grizzly bear, particularly before the introduction of firearms, was an act of raw courage that assured the reputation of the victorious hunter.

The grizzly also resembled humans in many ways, particularly with its habit of standing upright on its hind legs. A number of tribes believed the bear possessed supernatural powers and that it had the ability to transmute itself into human form. The bear was their most powerful guardian spirit and figured prominently in the traditions and ceremonies recorded by early travellers and ethnologists.

White fur traders, explorers, and travellers exhibited as much fear and respect for the power of the grizzly as Natives did, but not the same spiritual reverence. They either gave the animals a wide berth or, throwing caution to the winds, blasted away with inadequate firearms with the hope of securing a trophy. The outcome of these encounters was usually a toss-up; many hunters ended up fleeing for their lives from a wounded bear, or being mauled and mutilated. The stories of these early hunts were usually suspenseful, dramatic, and sometimes humourous, particularly if both bear and hunter escaped unscathed.

During the construction of the Canadian Pacific Railway, numerous black bears along the railroad were a target for anyone with access to a gun, and since firearms were becoming more powerful and reliable, there was less reluctance to hunt grizzly bears.

By the turn of the century, large areas of the central Canadian Rockies had been protected within national parks. While predators like wolves, coyotes, cougar, and lynx were considered undesirable animals and shot on sight, bears were among the protected species.

Early tourists wanted to see bears, but the chances of seeing them in the wild were often slim. As a result, captive black bears—usually orphaned cubs—were kept on chains outside hotels and business establishments in the resort centres of Banff, Field, Golden, and Rogers Pass. Though this practice was eventually discouraged by park authorities, it was soon replaced by the feeding of wild bears and enticement with garbage. Outlying hotels drew black bears to strategically-placed garbage dumps for visitor entertainment and photographs. As park townsites grew, village garbage dumps became popular viewing areas for bears, and once bears became accustomed to people and garbage, they started prowling townsite streets and alleys in their quest for food.

As early as 1916, park wardens and superintendents in Banff and Jasper recognized garbage-habituated bears as one of their most serious management problems. But people loved bears, and bears who begged for food by the roadside or scrapped and boxed with each other in a landfill site were far more entertaining than bears eating berries off in the woods. Of course, there was often disruption and destruction when a garbage bear invaded a hotel or work camp kitchen, but once the mess was cleaned up, one was left with yet another entertaining bear story.

Local residents accumulated these stories and passed them along to the tourists, and soon bear stories were as big a part of the national park experience as actually seeing the animals themselves. Many of these early stories recounted actual events, but eventually outfitters and tour guides started fabricating their own amazing tales to test the gullibility of the dudes. Tall tales gradually evolved into the bear joke, a story that kept listeners on the edge of their seats until the final line—the "kicker"—when they suddenly discovered they'd been had.

Park warden bear stories were often not as amusing. It was their duty to deal with aggressive garbage bears, usually looking down the sights of their rifles. And when grizzly bears acquired a taste for human food, things really got exciting. Garbage-habituated grizzlies saw any building as a potential source of food, and unattended warden cabins were a favourite target. Unlike their black cousins, these powerful, heavily-clawed animals could easily smash through a heavy door or rip a roof apart to gain entry. By mid-century, park wardens had all but declared war on these ursine invaders, and dozens of grizzlies were blasted to eternity by their supposed protectors. Warden stories from this period were often humorous and self-deprecating, always exciting, and usually tragic from the bear's point of view.

Following World War II, auto campers and campgrounds proliferated, as did exciting stories of bears breaking into vehicles and raiding tents. There was also an increasing number of bear attacks as more and more people entered grizzly country on foot. By the 1970s, wardens were spending much of their time relocating and destroying aggressive bears. Attitudes began to change during this period as conservationist-writers, like Andy Russell and Sid Marty, related a more compassionate style of bear story, and people began to realize that bears were not a limitless resource.

Since 1980, national and provincial park managers have worked hard and effectively to keep bears and garbage separate. They have developed bear-proof garbage containers; landfill sites have been closed and garbage is trucked beyond the mountains for disposal; and strict regulations are enforced concerning the feeding of wildlife, and the storage and disposal of human food in towns and campgrounds. Since most park bears no longer regard people as food providers, there are fewer close encounters with bears than in the past, which has resulted in fewer bear stories.

People still see bears grazing on vegetation along the roadside or in the backcountry, and there are still unexpected meetings on the trail that precipitate a bluff charge, a mauling, and the rare fatality, but these are far less frequent than in the past. So, mine may be the last generation with bags of bear stories.

The stories selected for this anthology are primarily from Canada's Rocky Mountains, although I have included a handful from the nearby Columbia Mountains in British Columbia. They were chosen primarily for their entertainment value, but they also reflect the changing attitudes toward bears, from the period of first contact with Native peoples to recent times. Bears have always symbolized the wilderness, and our changing attitudes towards them has been an indicator of how we feel about wild country.

Of course, one of our fascinations with bear stories is the desire to understand bear behaviour, in the hopes we can operate safely in the wild. Many stories in this book do reinforce the generally-accepted knowledge of how bears normally behave when they meet people, but many others confirm their unpredictability. Sometimes bears do the darnedest things.

If there is a lesson to be learned from these stories, it is to avoid surprise encounters with bears, which is sometimes easier said than done. It puts me in mind of one of my favourite bear stories, which occurred while swapping bear stories over coffee with park warden Billy Vroom about twenty years ago at the Banff Café. We'd been trading tales of close encounters with grizzly bears for the better part of half an hour, when Billy tried to come up with a reassuring observation.

"Well, you know, there's lots of places you can go in this park and not run into a bear."

We both fell silent and peered into our empty coffee cups, trying hard to think where that might be. Finally, Billy broke the silence.

"Like here in the Banff Café."

I
SPIRIT OF THE BEAR
Native Legends and Stories

Behold my nose with its keen scent,
My claws and teeth, they are my weapons.
Everything that lives fears the grizzly bear.

— from the Blackfoot legend of the Bear Spear —

THE BEAR LODGE

John C. Ewers

ACCORDING to Peigan tradition some of the oldest painted lodges are the bear ones. Their origin is explained in the following legend: Long ago a young Peigan determined to obtain some secret power which would bring him success in war. While traveling through heavy timber in search of a fasting place, he came upon a cave. He entered it. When his eyes became accustomed to the darkness he saw the cave was occupied by a mother bear and her cubs. When he pleaded with the bear mother not to harm him, she quieted down and even let him fondle her cubs. For four days and nights he stayed in the bear's den without food or water. Meanwhile he prayed to the bear to give him of its power.

On the fourth night he fell asleep. In his dream a male and female bear appeared. They took pity upon him. The female bear gave him her home, a handsome lodge with three red bears painted on each side and red circles on the front and back representing the bears' den. The doorway was covered with a bearskin. She also gave him incense to be burned in the lodge day and night, a blackstone pipe bowl carved in the shape of a bear, and a song, "Underneath there is a bear which is very powerful. With her protection I shall always be spared in battle."

Then the male bear spoke. "My son, I give you my lodge too." Two black bears standing on their hind legs were painted on this lodge, one at each side of the entrance. The father bear also gave him a pipe and a drum.

Then the mother bear gave him a knife with a bear-jaw handle. She threw the knife at him, and he grabbed it before it could harm him. The bears gave him a song to go with it. "A knife is just like dirt thrown against me."

The bears then drove their children back into the brush and painted themselves. They painted their faces red and made long vertical stripes on their faces by scratching off the paint with their claws.

They told him, "This is how you should paint for battle. This painting will protect you."

When enemies of the bears came through the brush and attacked them, the male bear charged and killed the attackers. Then he told the boy, "See. That is the way. Always charge in battle as I just did."

The next day the young man left the bears' den. Not long afterward he joined a war party. In battle he carried a bear knife, painted himself, and charged as the bears had taught him. He took several scalps, but was himself unharmed. After he returned home, he made the two bear lodges just as the bears had shown them to him in his dream.

LEGEND OF THE BEAR SPEAR

Onesta (Blackfoot)

as recorded by Walter McClintock

*T*HE things I now tell you happened long ago, in the days when our people used dogs instead of horses to carry their baggage. One evening, when a band of Indians came into camp, the chief announced that one of his travois dogs was lost. No one remembered seeing the dog, so Little Mink, youngest son of the chief, asked his father to let him go back to look for the missing dog. He said:

"I am old enough to make the trip alone. I shall go straight to our old camp-ground."

At first the father refused, he thought his son was too young to make such a long trip alone. But the boy was so eager, he was allowed to go.

Little Mink followed the trail back to their last camp-ground, which was close to the foot of the Rocky Mountains. First he went to the place where his father's lodge had stood; he thought the dog might still be there. Then he walked around the deserted camp-circle, watching the ground for tracks.

At last he found a single dog track going towards the mountains. It led him into a well-worn trail through a rocky ravine, to a cave whose mouth was hidden by service-berry and chokecherry bushes. And there he saw the missing travois, but the dog was gone.

While Little Mink was looking at the travois and wondering what had become of their dog, he heard a loud roar; and a big grizzly bear rushed from the cave. Raising himself on his hind legs, he seized the boy in his arms and carried him into the dark cave. When Little Mink's eyes became accustomed to the dark, and he saw the enormous size of the bear that held him, he fainted. After a while he wakened and found himself lying on the floor of the cave, so close to the mouth of the big grizzly he could feel his hot breath. When he tried to move, the bear thrust out his long sharp claws and held him tight. After that the boy lay very still; he scarcely even moved, but gazed straight ahead. At last the bear said:

"My son, be not afraid, for I shall do you no harm. I am the chief of the bears and my power is very great. It was my power that brought you to this cave. If you are willing to remain here with me while the snows are deep, I will help you. Before you leave my den in the spring, I will bestow my power upon you. You will become a great chief and can help your people."

Then the grizzly stood upon his hind legs; he was so big his head almost touched the roof. First he walked round and round; and showed the boy a pile of green branches with different kinds of berries. He said:

"You will have plenty of berries for food. The bear eats them branches and all, but you can pick off the berries."

After that the bear took him to the other side of the cave and showed him a pile of buffalo chips. He changed these into pemmican through his supernatural power, dancing around the cave and holding them in his paws.

All that winter Little Mink stayed in the cave with the bear, acting just as he did. His eyes became so accustomed to the dark, he could see as well as the bear himself. While the snow was deep, the bear lay on one side, he did not even move. But, when the warm winds of spring began to blow, he began to get restless and move about. One day the bear rolled over on his back and lay for a long time with his legs in the air. He sat up and began to yawn. Then he rose to his feet and walked round and round the cave, and finally stopped to look outside.

He said that spring had come and it was time to leave the cave. He took the boy to the door and told him to look out. A warm wind was blowing and the snow was melting from the hills. But, before they left the den, the grizzly bestowed some of his supernatural power upon Little Mink.

He took a stick and raised himself on his hind legs, holding out his arms and extending his long claws. He tossed up his huge head and snorted and rolled back his lips; he showed his sharp teeth and chanted:

> Behold my nose with its keen scent,
> My claws and teeth, they are my weapons.
> Everything that lives fears the grizzly bear.

And then the bear said to Little Mink:

"When you get back to your tribe, make a Bear Spear. Take a sharp stone and fasten it to a long shaft. Fasten bear's teeth to the handle, also the nose of a bear, because the nose and teeth should go together. Cover the staff with bearskin and decorate it with red paint. Tie grizzly claws to the handle; they will rattle and sound like a grizzly does when he runs. Whenever you go to war, wear the claw of a grizzly bear fastened in your hair; and my power will go with you. Make a noise like a grizzly bear when you charge in battle; and your enemies will run, because everything that lives fears the power of a grizzly bear."

The bear taught Little Mink how to heal the sick. He showed him the ceremony to use; how to paint his face and body and the marks to use for the 'bear face.' He told him that the Spear was sacred and should be used only on important occasions. If any one were ill, a relative could make a vow to the Bear Spear. After that the ceremony should be given, and the sick would be restored.

Then Little Mink left the grizzly and returned to his father's camp. The chief was proud of his son. He gave a big feast and invited the head men to meet him. After they had feasted and smoked, Little Mink told them how he spent the winter in the den of the chief of the grizzly bears and showed his Bear Spear.

THE NURTURING BEAR

Flathead Tale

paraphrased by David Rockwell

While they feared the power of the grizzly bear, Kootenay and Interior Salish peoples believed these animals could be benevolent to humans. They believed grizzly bears could bestow their power upon people and provide guardian spirits for worthy individuals. Women were often recipients of this gift, undoubtedly because of an association with the powerful maternal instincts displayed by mother bears.

A Flathead woman named Sdipp-Shin-Mah (Fallen from the sky) relates a tale of how "the grizzly spirit gave me its power"—a story reflecting Native appreciation for the nurturing character of the mother bear and a belief that bears could readily change back and forth from animal to human form.

ONE day when I was a girl just about six or seven winters, my mother told me we were going berrying in the mountains. We rode double on her horse and went high into the mountains. It was getting late in the evening. I saw a patch of bushes. I told my mother, "Look, there are some berries and plenty of them."

She said, "Child have patience, a little farther up is the place where we will get our berries."

So we went on and on until when the sun was just about going down she stopped our horse and said, "Here is the place where we are going to pick."

She put me off the horse and got off also. She started picking and put some berries on the ground for me and said, "Sit here and eat on these berries while I go down here to see if there are more below."

She spread out my robe, and I sat on it and began eating. She got on the horse and reminded me to stay where I was, and she said she would be back soon. She disappeared in the bushes. I was not afraid. I ate berries and talked to myself about the trees. Then I saw night was coming and my mother was not yet back. I became frightened and called for her. I called for my mother but saw no sign of her. I called and called while crying, not knowing what to do. I just cried and cried and called for my mother all night. But there was no use. She had left me and went back home leaving me alone in the high mountains.

When I could not cry any longer, I got up and took my robe and walked not knowing where I was going. It was still night and very dark. I went on until I got tired and sleepy and lay down and went to sleep. When I woke up the sun was way up already, and it was nice and warm. At first I thought I was sleeping with my mother at home. Then I remembered I was high in the mountains, and my mother was not there. I started to cry again. When I stopped crying I began to walk and eat the berries growing there. I kept on until I got to a deep gulch fully covered with trees. While I sat there I thought of my home and my mother. I began to cry again. Then I heard a sound that I thought was human voices. I listened closely but heard nothing and thought it must be the cry of a bird or something. Then I heard a sound again, and as I listened I heard it again and again and knew it was the sound of humans laughing and talking loudly way down in the bottom of the gulch. I could not see them as it was covered all over with trees and bushes, but I could tell they were coming toward me.

Just where I was sitting on a ridge and below on the hillside was an open bald place. The sound came from that way and I was watching closely and was surprised with joy to see a woman with two little ones coming. I thought it was someone from my tribe. They were running and chasing each other. Laughing and shouting, they came pretty close. I saw the woman was a very handsome woman, well clothed all in buckskin, and clean. One of the children was a boy and one was a girl. They were also well dressed, all in buckskin.

This woman said to me, "Poor girl, this is not the place for you especially to be alone. I am sure you are thirsty by this time. Come, we will bring you down to the stream to drink." Then she told her children, "Do not bother your little sister, she is thirsty and tired."

While we were going down, the children were playing and laughing and tried to get me to play with them but the mother always stopped them saying, "Your little sister is tired so leave her alone."

When we got to the stream we all had a good drink. I was last to finish my drink and when I stood and looked, instead of seeing my little sister and brother and mother there was sitting there a grizzly bear and two cubs. I was afraid. The bear spoke, "Do not be afraid, little child. I am your mother bear and here is your little brother and sister. We will not hurt you."

Then she told me this: "Listen closely. I am going to give you medicine power by which you will be a great help to your people in the future. This time will come after you pass middle age. But do not try to do more than I am allowing you or granting you because, if you do, it will be nothing more than false and you will be responsible for sufferings and even death. One of my gifts is that you are going to be helpful to women especially those that are having hard times and suffering giving the birth of a child." She said this. Then the grizzly bear mother and her cubs took me back to my people.

A STONEY BEAR STORY

Walter Wilcox

The following story was related to the mountaineer-explorer Walter Wilcox by the Stoney Indians near the end of the nineteenth century.

A young brave named Susie was encamped with his family in the Porcupine Hills east of the Rockies. After hunting sheep and goats all day, he was returning to his teepee and upon entering an open forest glade came unexpectedly on a huge grizzly bear. He fired, though too quickly for good aim, and only wounded the bear in the fore foot. Walking backwards, and trying to get another cartridge in his rifle, he stumbled on a log and fell. The bear jumped upon him before he could recover. Then ensued a fight to the death. The Indian turned on his side and seized the bear's ear with his left hand. In the other he held his Hudson Bay hunting-knife, a formidable weapon like a small sword, and with this kept striking the bear on the face and neck. Biting and clawing, the infuriated animal reared on his hind legs several times in an effort to throw the Indian from him. At length both contestants, weakened from loss of blood, fell to the ground, when Susie, with a desperate effort, drove the knife between the bear's shoulders, but had no strength to pull the weapon out. Maddened with pain, the bear gave his head a great toss and threw the Indian several yards to one side.

On the following morning Susie's people began to search for him. Within a few yards of the dead bear the Indian was found and carried back to camp. There they dressed his wounds and roasted the feet of the grizzly, that he might eat them and become a mighty hunter, for by eating the bear's feet the spirit of the animal would enter and give him courage. When asked what he thought about while the fight was going on he said: "I was thinking—why is a bear's ear not long like a deer's?"

HECTOR CRAWLER
AND THE BEAR

George McLean (Stoney)

as recorded by Marius Barbeau

Hector Crawler was a respected chief and medicine man of the Stoney nation. George McLean's story relates one of the chief's adventures just prior to the coming of the railroad.

W HEN Hector Crawler was young, he was a great hunter and trapper. He went trapping to the mountains on snowshoes every year in the spring. And I have followed him a couple of times. We packed our grub, maybe fifty pounds of flour on our backs, and our bedding. When camping time would come, he would hunt where there was shelter of trees and not too much sun, because up in the mountains there was five or ten feet of snow. We used to cut boughs off the trees for bedding on top of the snow and then make a fire. Crawler took all these trips.

One day in the summer, just below the place now called Banff where the CPR crosses the Bow River, there was a bear on the other side of the Bow River. Another man with Crawler was Gahimangku (Crows-Breast). He told him, "Let us go and play with the bear!" It was a big grizzly. They had guns with them. But they just wanted to make fun, and let it be known that they were capable and brave enough to tackle a grizzly with just one gun. They stripped off their clothes. Hector had a big knife, one of these big Hudson's Bay knives. He put that knife behind his back, into his belt. But Gahimangku had no knife. Just as they were doing this, the bear came into the river. They went into the river too, also to meet him. And just as they got in the middle of the river, they

23

met the bear swimming and got on each side of it. When the bear wanted to grab at one man, the other would grab the bear and turn him, while swimming. They played with him like that until they had floated maybe half a mile down stream. The river became shallow. There they could swim no longer. But the bear still could swim. Then Crawler took his knife and thrust it into its side. He gave the knife to his friend, who did the same. And they let the bear go. It floated along and died. And they got it to the shore. And then they skinned it and took the meat. This is the story of these hunters, of what they did to the bear.

In November 1896, eleven years following the completion of the CPR, Hector Crawler and his family were returning across the mountains through heavy snow from a trip to the Kootenay Valley. When they reached the Bow Valley, the party was following the snowless tracks of the railway when a train came upon them suddenly. Crawler's family managed to escape into the heavy snow on either side of the tracks, but the chief was injured and many of his horses were killed. It was said that Crawler never fully recovered from the loss.

"THINGS ARE CHANGING"

Ella E. Clark

from a story by William Gingrass (Kootenay)

ONE time when the Kutenais were having their usual troubles with the Blackfeet, a band of our people were camping in the mountains. The leader of the band was named Sowatts.

Sowatts decided one morning that he would go out and get some fresh meat. He was warned that he might run into Grizzly Bear and was reminded that someone in the band had disobeyed the bear's instructions.

Grizzly Bear had charge of all plants, roots, and berries, and he forbade people to eat certain of them. "Some plants belong to animals," he said. "Human beings are forbidden to eat them." The first thing a boy or girl was taught was to avoid eating certain plants. Grizzly Bear had also taught the women how to cook plants—for example, how to steam camas roots.

Not long before this, some person had eaten a plant that belonged to the animals. So when Grizzly Bear met Sowatts alone in the mountains, he tore the man's hair out, pulled his arms off—tore him to pieces.

Three days later his people found him dead. They carried his body back to camp, planning to bury it in the shale the next morning. But he came back to life. He had no hair and no lips. It was difficult for him to talk, but people could see that he had something he wanted to say to them. "Tomorrow I will tell you," he managed to make clear.

After sunrise the next morning, he said to them, "Things are changing. While I was with the spirits, after Grizzly Bear killed me, they took me to the top of a mountain. When we looked toward the place where the sun rises, we saw many people. They were not dressed like us. One man I noticed in particular was dressed in a black robe.

"The spirit chief said to me, 'See that man? He is the one who will take over when we spirits are gone. We have done all we can for you and your people. That man will come some time in the next ten snows. Before he comes other people will come with the same words, but not dressed like him. Let them pass through.'

"Today," continued Sowatts, "you must turn back and go forth to make peace with the Blackfeet. The spirits can no longer help us."

But some people in the camp did not want to believe Sowatts.

"Give us proof," they said to him. "Give us some proof that what you say is right."

"Prove it by killing Grizzly Bear," said another. "He is now near our camp. He runs in, scares the children, and then hides in the brush where we can not see him and kill him."

Sowatts called his dog, "Now go over to that brush and get that bear out so that the men can kill him."

The dog rolled over three times and then jumped into the brush. Soon the bear ran out and the men killed him. All the people then believed Sowatts. They made peace with the Blackfeet, and the following year the Kutenais went to their country and exchanged gifts with them.

A few snows later a missionary and his wife came among the Kutenais, stopping at Nyak. They had some message, but the Indians paid no attention to them. Later Father De Smet came and started a mission.

From that time on, the Indians began to lose their power. The spirits had deserted them.

II

EARLY BEAR TALES
Fur Traders, Explorers, and Travellers

THE FIRST BEAR STORY

David Thompson

In the autumn of 1787, David Thompson travelled with a party of Hudson's Bay Company traders to winter with the Peigan Indians in the foothills of the Rockies southwest of present-day Calgary. Thompson and one of his companions were billeted in the tent of an old Cree who had lived with the Peigans for many decades. Shortly after arriving in the camp, the traders observed a tragic episode when three Native boys tried to prove their manhood by killing a grizzly bear. Thompson's account is the earliest description of a grizzly bear attack in the Rocky Mountains.

A few days after our arrival, the death cry was given, and the Men all started out of the Tents, and our old tent mate with his gun in his hand. The cry was from a young man who held his Bow and Arrows, and showed one of his thighs torn by a grizled bear, and which had killed two of his companions. The old Man called for his powder horn and shot bag, and seeing the priming of his gun in good order, he set off with the young man for the Bear, which was at a short distance. They found him devouring one of the dead. The moment he saw them he sat up on his hind legs, showing them his teeth and long clawed paws, in this, his usual position, to defend his prey, his head is a bad mark, but his breast offers a direct mark to the heart, through which the old Man sent his ball and killed him. The two young men who were destroyed by the Bear, had each, two iron shod Arrows, and the camp being near, they attacked the bear for his skin and claws. But unfortunately their arrows stuck in the bones of his ribs, and only irritated him; he sprung on the first, and with one of his dreadful fore paws tore out his bowels and three of his ribs; the second he seized in his paws, and almost crushed him to death, threw him down, when the third Indian hearing their cries came to their assistance and sent an arrow which only wounded him in the neck, for which the Bear chased him, and slightly tore one of his thighs. The first poor fellow was still alive and knew his parents, in whose arms he expired. The Bear, for the mischief he had done was condemned to be burnt to ashes, the claws of his fore paws, very sharp and long, the young man wanted for a collar but it was not granted; those that burned the Bear watched until nothing but ashes remained. The two young men were each wrapped up separately in Bison robes, laid side by side on the ground, and covered with logs of wood and stones.

GRIZZLY ATTACKS ON THE FRASER RIVER

Simon Fraser

In July 1806, Simon Fraser and a party of North West Company traders crossed the Arctic-Pacific watershed divide to explore the river that would one day bear Fraser's name. There they experienced two particularly bad days with bears. Fraser's journal entries show how the Natives understood the value of playing dead during a grizzly attack.

SUNDAY, July 13 ... About 4 P.M., as we were advancing inside of an Island, we saw two [bear] cubs in a tree and immediately pulled ashore to fire upon them, but before we could get to them they were off, and La Garde and Barbuellen, who were the first on shore, pursued them. The latter soon met the mother and fired upon her to no effect, and she pursued him in her turn, but he being near the water he jumped in, and she after him, but soon left him, and as La Garde was advancing another Bear suddenly rushed upon him and tore him in a shocking manner. Had not the dogs passed there at that critical moment, he would have been torn to pieces. The Bear left him to defend herself against the dogs, and during the interval he ran off and jumped into the River, and from thence it was with much difficulty he could walk to the canoe. He received nine or ten bad wounds and we encamped early to dress them. We are really unfortunate in regard to the men. One of the canoes will be now obliged to continue with three, and no great help can be expected. The Indians (except the Montagne de boutte who returned to encamp with us, on account of his having his son on board the canoe) are ahead.

Monday, July 14. It was rather late before we set off, on account of our having La Garde ['s] wounds to dress before our departure. At 9 A.M. we came to an Indian house that was situated on the end of an Island, and opposite on the right shore there were two tombs neatly erected. There we breakfasted, and from thence soon got to a long Rapid, where we were obliged to unload and carry one half of the loads, and put the people of both canoes upon [in one?], to take them up one after another, which nearly occupied the remainder of the day; and by the time that the canoes were gummed and ready to be off, the sun was near set. However, we set off and encamped about two miles above the Rapid.

As Tabah Tha and his wife were walking along the banks of the River, they surprissed a large grizzly bear and her two cubs. The Indian fired upon the mother and wounded her, in revenge of which she jumped upon his wife, and she instantly laid down flat upon the ground and did not stir, in consequence of [which] the bear deserted [her] and ran after her husband, who likewise fortunately escaped unhurt and killed one of the young, which he brought back to the canoe. He was immediately sent back with other Indians in search of the one he wounded, which they found and killed with seven shots, and brought the meat to the canoe, which made all hands a couple of good meals.

THE BOTANIST AND THE BEAR

Thomas Drummond

Thomas Drummond was the first botanist to visit the Canadian Rockies when he wintered in the Athabasca Valley in 1826–1827. During his stay in the mountains and foothills, he had numerous close encounters with grizzly bears, undoubtedly because he often travelled alone and on foot in his quest for botanical specimens. The following incident near Jasper House initiated his education in bear behaviour.

I agreed to accompany the brigade as far as Jasper's House, and accordingly set out with them on horseback. Having crossed the Assinaboyne River, the party halted to breakfast, and I went on before them for a few miles, to procure specimens of a *Jungermannia*, which I had previously observed in a small rivulet on our track. On this occasion I had a narrow escape from the jaws of a grisly bear; for, while passing through a small open glade, intent upon discovering the moss of which I was in search, I was surprised by hearing a sudden rush and then a harsh growl, just behind me; and on looking round, I beheld a large bear approaching towards me, and two young ones making off in a contrary direction as fast as possible. My astonishment was great, for I had not calculated upon seeing these animals so early in the season, and this was the first I had met with. She halted within two or three yards of me, growling and rearing herself on her hind feet, then suddenly wheeled about, and went off in the direction the young ones had taken, probably to ascertain whether they were safe. During this momentary absence, I drew from my gun the small shot with which I had been firing at ducks during the morning, and which, I was well aware, would avail me nothing against so large and powerful a creature, and replaced it with ball. The bear, meanwhile, had advanced and retreated two or three times, apparently more furious than ever; halting at each interval within a shorter and shorter distance of me, always raising herself on her hind legs, and growling a horrible defiance, and at length approaching to within the length of my gun from me. Now was my time to fire: but judge of my alarm and mortification, when I found that my gun would not go off! The morning had been wet, and the damp had communicated to the powder. My only resource was to plant myself firm and stationary, in the hope of disabling the bear by a blow on her head with the butt end of my gun, when she should throw herself on me to seize me. She had gone and returned ten or a dozen times, her rage apparently increasing with her additional confidence, and I momentarily expected to find myself in her gripe, when the dogs belonging to the brigade made their appearance, but on beholding the bear they fled with all possible speed. The horsemen were just behind, but such was the surprise and alarm of the whole party, that though there were several hunters and at least half-a-dozen guns among them, the bear made her escape unhurt, passing one of the horsemen, (whose gun, like mine, missed fire,) and apparently intimidated by the number of the party. For the future, I took care to keep my gun in better order, but I found, by future experience, that the best mode of getting rid of the bears when attacked by them, was to rattle my vasculum, or specimen box, when they immediately decamp. This is the animal described by Lewis and Clark in their *Travels on the Missouri*, and so much dreaded by the Indians. My adventure with the bear did not, however, prevent my accomplishing the collecting of the *Jungermannia*. It is No. 17 of the "American Mosses."

MR. O'B. AND THE THREE BEARS

Viscount Milton and W.B. Cheadle

British travellers Viscount Milton and Dr. W.B. Cheadle journeyed from Edmonton House to the Rocky Mountains in June of 1863 with their guide Baptiste Supernat and a Métis family, which consisted of a man they called "The Assiniboine," his wife, and son. Also along for the ride was an itinerant, middle-aged Irish cleric named Felix O'Byrne—"Mr. O'B."

M R. O'B. was a man of the most marvellous timidity. His fears rendered his life a burden to him. But of all the things he dreaded—and their name was legion—his particular horror was a grisly bear. On this point he was a complete monomaniac. He had never yet seen a grisly bear, but he was in the daily expectation of meeting one of these terrible animals, and a sanguinary and untimely end at the same time. As he walked through the forest, the rustle of every leaf and the creaking of the trunks seemed, to his anxious mind, to herald the approach of his dreaded enemy. The Assiniboine, taking advantage of his weakness, cured him for a time of his carelessness in losing sight of the party, by lying in wait, hid amongst the trees close to the track, and as Mr. O'B. passed by, set up a most horrible growling, which caused him to take to his heels incontinently, and for several days he kept near protection. As we sat round the camp-fire one evening, a rustling in the bushes attracted our attention, and we were startled for a moment by the sight of a dark, shaggy object moving along, which, in the dim, fitful fire-light, looked very like a bear. Mr. O'B. rushed up to us in abject terror, when the animal, passing into clearer view, disclosed a foot clothed in a moccasin, and we recognised the boy, enveloped in a buffalo robe, and creeping on all fours, to practise on the fears of "Le Vieux."

On the third day after leaving Pembina River, we rested to dine at a marshy meadow formed by the damming up of the stream by beaver, exactly similar to those we noticed near Dog River and at Edmonton. But now these places were of the greatest value to us, for they afforded almost the only open grassy spaces we found with pasturage for our horses until reaching the mountains ...

On the evening of this same day we encamped early in a little open space on the bank of a small stream, one of the very few we met with in this part. Cheadle and The Assiniboine started up the river in search of beaver, but the former, seeing some trout rising, turned back in order to fish for them, and The Assiniboine went on alone. The camp was made, Cheadle came in at dark with some fish, and we had supper. Mr. O'B. went to bed, and the rest sat smoking and wondering what made The Assiniboine so late, when the door of the lodge was lifted, and he entered, literally trembling with excitement, and for some time hardly able to explain the cause, merely saying, in his French patois, "J'etais en pas mal de danger. J'ai vu les our gris, proche—proche!" and devoted himself to smoking a pipe, which his son immediately filled and handed to him. When sufficiently calmed down by the composing weed, he related his adventures. He had found beaver up the stream and shot one, which sank, and he was unable to secure it. Wandering on for some time without meeting with anything more, he turned back, just before dusk, and retraced his steps. When he arrived within a few hundred yards of the camp, he heard a rustling in some underwood near by, and thinking the horses had strayed there, turned aside into the cover to drive them back. Instead of seeing the horses he expected, he found himself face to face with an enormous grisly bear, which was engaged in tearing open a rotten trunk in search of insects. On the appearance of The Assiniboine, the animal desisted from its employment, and advanced towards him with a terrible growling and lips upcurled, displaying her great teeth and enormous mouth. The first bear was now joined by two others of rather smaller size, who came running up, attracted by the growling. The Assiniboine, an old and practised hunter, stood his ground firmly, and as the old bear came within two or three yards, suddenly threw up his arms. This, a usual device in hunting the grisly bear, caused the animal to stop for a moment and sit up on her hind legs, giving an opportunity for a steady shot. The Assinboine took a deliberate aim, and pulled the trigger, but, to his dismay, the snapping of the cap only followed. He pulled the second trigger, and that missed fire also. Strange to say, the bear did not attack him, and as he continued to show a firm and immovable front, retired with the others, and all three stood watching him. At every attempt he made to move, one or other rushed towards him, growling fiercely. This continued for some time, but at length they resumed their occupation of breaking up the rotten logs, and he stole off unperceived. He was not, however, content to leave them undisturbed after his narrow escape. When well out of sight he stopped, poured fresh powder into the nipples of his gun, and re-capped it. He then crept cautiously round, so as to approach them from an opposite quarter. He found them still in the same place, occupied as before. Crouching behind a natural barricade of fallen trees, he took a fair deliberate shot at the old bear. Again both barrels missed fire, and the three, aroused by the snapping of the caps, looked round, and quickly perceiving him, rushed up, growling and showing their teeth, but stopped as they came to the barrier of trees, which they fortunately made no attempt to pass. The same scene previously described was now re-enacted, the animals resenting any sign which the man showed of retiring, but refraining from actual attack. At last they all suddenly set off at speed, and after a time The Assiniboine reached the camp without further molestation. The man probably owed his life to his courageous bearing, and the circumstance that his gun missed fire, for had he wounded one of them, all three would certainly have attacked and, undoubtedly, killed him.

Whilst The Assiniboine was relating his exciting adventure, Mr. O'B. lay rolled in his blanket, quite unconscious that anything unusual had occurred, not understanding a word of the mixed patois of Cree and French in which The Assiniboine spoke. Milton therefore said in English, "Mr. O'B., The Assiniboine has been attacked by three grisly bears, close to camp." At the word *bears* he sat bolt upright, his countenance betraying the greatest anxiety, and eagerly asked if it was really true, and how it happened. We told him the story, and as he listened his jaw fell ruefully, and his face assumed an agonised expression. "Doctor," said he, when we had finished, "it's no use shutting our eyes to the fact; we are in a most serious position—in very great danger. Jamdiu expectans expectavi! This is a most terrible journey; will you do me a great favour, and lend me your revolver? for I am resolved to sell my life dearly, and how can I defend myself if the bears attack us in the night? I'm an unarmed man."

"Oh, certainly," replied Cheadle, producing the pistol, and playfully working the hammer up and down with his thumb; "with the greatest pleasure; here it is: oh, yes, if you like: perhaps, under the circumstances, you had better take it; but I ought to tell you that you must be extremely careful with it, for it is in the habit of going off of its own accord."

Mr. O'B. hastily drew back his hand stretched out to take the pistol, considered—hesitated—and at last decided that perhaps he had better not meddle with so dangerous a weapon. He contented himself with taking the large axe to bed with him, although it may be doubted whether he would have used it very effectually if occasion had required. We were all much excited at The Assiniboine's story, and at once resolved to go in pursuit of the bears at daybreak next morning.

As soon as it became light we prepared for the hunt. The woman and boy were to accompany us in order to search for the beaver which The Assiniboine had killed the night before, Mr. O'B., to his infinite dismay, being left alone in charge of the camp. He remonstrated strongly, and dilated upon the probability of the bears taking advantage of our absence to attack the undefended position. Finding we were inflexible, "Delirant reges, plectuntur Achivi," said Mr. O'B. disconsolately, and immediately retired within the lodge, let down the door, made up a tremendous fire to scare away the enemy, and remained seated, with the axe by his side, in anxious expectation until our return. We proceeded under the guidance of The Assiniboine to the scene of his adventure the previous evening. There we found every detail of his narrative confirmed—the rotten trunks torn asunder, the huge footprints of the bears in the soft soil or long grass, worn into a beaten track where they had so repeatedly charged up to him, his own track as he took the circuitous route to his second position behind the logs; and leading away from the place, the marks of the three bears going off at speed. It appeared, however, that they had not left the neighbourhood until that morning, for we found very fresh tracks crossing the stream, and on the opposite bank, a wet line marked by the drippings from the shaggy coats of the animals after emerging from the water.

We followed on, The Assiniboine leading, at a great pace, yet with wonderful stillness, through the thick underwood, finding from time to time fresher and still fresher signs—a rotten log newly torn open, a bees' nest just dug up, and footmarks in which the grass seemed still rising after the removal of the pressure. We were in a high state of excitement, stealthily advancing, with guns cocked and bated breath, expecting every moment to see their terrible forms close to us, when we came upon a hard, grassless stretch of ground, where the men were unable to follow the tracks, and, after a long search, were, much to our chagrin, compelled to give up the pursuit.

Milton and Baptiste returned to camp to pack up and proceed on the journey, Cheadle and Assiniboine being bent on following a fresh moose-track which we had crossed. They rejoined the party before nightfall, without having succeeded in finding the animal they had followed.

When Milton arrived near the camp, he observed Mr. O'B.'s head cautiously protruded from the lodge door, taking an observation, and when he perceived that human beings, and not bears, were approaching, he ventured forth, welcoming them with great glee, and discoursing on the dreadful suspense he had endured during their absence.

On the following day, when Cheadle was about to start ahead of the party, for the sake of meeting with game, Mr. O'B. warned him to be very careful, advising him to load both barrels with ball, and carry his gun on full cock, ready for emergency. Cheadle, however, told him it was necessary to have one barrel loaded with small shot for the feathered game, and marched off laughing, Mr. O'B. looking after him with an expression of pity, and shaking his head ominously. Milton and the rest travelled on nearly the whole day, wondering that they did not find Cheadle at mid-day, as usual, waiting for them in some convenient camping ground. Cursing his folly for leading them so far, they at last pulled up in despair, and waited, in the belief that he must have lost his way. Mr. O'B., however, took a different view. "My lord," said he to Milton, "you may depend upon it the Doctor has met those bears. I've warned him repeatedly against the rashness of walking alone in this way. It was only this very morning, as you heard, I advised him to be careful, and load both barrels with ball. But he only laughed at me, and walked off with his gun on half-cock, carelessly thrown over his shoulder. And now you see the terrible consequences. Medicus ipse mortalis. There is not the slightest doubt that he has been surprised by those three bears, and torn to pieces, poor fellow!" Mr. O'B.'s prophecies of evil were, however, upset by the appearance of the missing man. He had lost his way in a series of swamps, and with some difficulty retraced his steps to the right track. Then he had a long, stern chase to catch the rest, who had, in the meantime, passed on before him.

MEMORIES OF A BEAR HUNTER

Henry J. Moberly

Henry John Moberly was first employed by the Hudson's Bay Company in 1854, and he worked off and on for the firm over the next forty years. In the 1860s he took a break from the company and set off on his own to hunt and trap in British Columbia's northern interior and the Rocky Mountains. There he became famous as a skilful bear hunter using a technique that required nerves of steel.

ON 1st June, 1864, I left the Hudson's Bay Company's service for the second time, handing over my charge to the clerk sent out to assume it. As my account could not be closed until received from Victoria I decided upon remaining at Fraser Lake for some hunting and fishing until August, when I could accompany the Hudson's Bay Company's boats going down to Fort Alexander on the Fraser River below Quesnelle. Here I should obtain my settlement.

In a small canoe, accompanied by a young Indian lad, I first hunted up the Nechaco River. My bag at our initial camp was five beaver. Next morning when about to fire at another beaver, at a sign from my boy I looked up to see a bear feeding on a hill some distance off. I recognized him as a two-year-old grizzly.

We landed and had approached rather close when two more came in view, a large female and her cub. My lad promptly declined to advance any nearer and made for the canoe. When within two hundred yards of them the female saw me, reared up and then commenced to walk slowly away. I hurried after her and she turned again, waiting for my next move. Seeing that I still advanced she dropped on all fours and came to meet me. I halted until she was within six feet of me and then threw my cap in her face. She reared again, and as she came down I pressed the trigger

41

and she rolled over, stone dead. I then shot the cub. The other had by this time disappeared.

I may here claim that few white men and not many Indians have killed more bears than myself, and I never risked firing at a grizzly from a farther distance than six or seven feet. I was often told I was foolhardy, but the truth is I was afraid to fire from a longer range. If a bear is wounded and makes a rush I defy any man to place an effective shot, for as the bear approaches his head swings from side to side. All the grizzly-hunting accidents I have ever seen or heard of have been due to firing first from too great a distance and crippling the animal only; then the beast closed with the hunter, and either badly mangled or killed him before he could administer the knockout shot.

If you meet a grizzly he will always rise once or twice on his hind legs. If on approaching and when within a couple of yards he doesn't stand erect, throw your guncoat, cap or anything at hand in his face, and he will always rise. As he comes down for the final rush take steady aim, and the man who misses the vital spot from that distance has no business to hunt bear and probably will never have another chance.

However, not all the bears he met fell for his foolproof system.

One chase after a grizzly gave two of us three days' hard work, with nothing to eat or drink but snow water.

The snow was about a foot deep, and I was hunting when late in the afternoon I came on the track of a bear. Next morning with a companion I went forth in pursuit of bruin, taking with me our blankets, tea kettle and food for one day. The bear had travelled farther than we had anticipated, but toward evening we came to a small round mountain on which we were certain we should find his den. We camped at the foot and no doubt the bear heard us, for it was a still night and bitterly cold. Next morning, as we were taking a turn round the hill, we started a moose and began firing at him. The range was too great, however, and he escaped.

The shooting must have decided the bear to shift his quarters, and when we again struck his track he probably had an hour or more the start of us. Off we set, expecting soon to overhaul him, but he led us into such frightful places—down such deep gulches, up such steep hills—that we never got near enough for a shot. When night came there was nothing for it but to camp, and without blankets or kettle, which we had left at the previous night's camp. We made the best of a tough situation by keeping a large fire well stoked until daybreak.

All next day we followed the bear, and all next night found our only solace in a big fire. The following day found us again on his track, determined to persevere to a finish.

About ten o'clock in the morning of the fourth day we caught sight of him at last, climbing a bare hill half a mile away. We put on steam and presently were overhauling him. The hill sloped down to the Pine River, and the chase began to get exciting. But the river was in our way, frozen only at the banks and open in the middle. When we reached the near bank it was only to see the bear climbing out on the opposite one, and here the chase ended.

We were eighteen miles from home, and when at last we reached it, it may easily be imagined that we were both hungry and disgruntled and ready enough to swear vengeance against all bears for the future.

ADVENTURES
ON THE CPR SURVEY

Robert M. Rylatt

Robert Rylatt was an employee of the CPR survey under British Columbia engineer Walter Moberly. During the summer of 1872, the survey party was ordered to move across the Rockies from the mouth of the Blaeberry to the Athabasca River. Bears were constant companions as the men worked their way north along the Columbia River en route to Athabasca Pass.

TUESDAY, August 20th. Poor old Chief Kimbasket has come to grief. He was in his place a day or two ago, or in other words was somewhat in advance of the party blazing the route, when of a sudden he was set upon by a bear, and having no arms save his light axe, his bearship took him at advantage; the rush to the attack was so sudden, and the animal apparently so furious, the old chief had barely time to raise the axe and aim a blow as the brute raired, 'ere his weapon was dashed aside like a flash, and he was in the embrace of the monster, the huge forepaws around him, the immense claws dug into his back, the bear held him up; then fastening the poor chiefs shoulder in his iron Jaws, he raised one of his hind feet, and tore a fearful gash; commencing at the abdomen, and cutting through to the bowels, he fairly stripped the flesh and muscles from one of his thighs, a bloody hanging mass of flesh and rent clothing. Thus he was found the following morning, being too weak and torn to attempt to reach camp. What a night of suffering he must have had. Green, who by the way has studied medicine, and is considerable of a doctor, says he hopes to bring him round all right, but that he has had a narrow squeek for it. As soon as he can travel, he will be sent off with the Indians who will shortly be leaving us.

Bruin may not be attacked with anything short of a Rifle, unless the hunter is tired of his life, and adopts this method of passing out of existence. A long keen blade may do the business, but the chances are in bruin's favour by long odds in a rough and tumble fight. He may be a clumsy looking animal, but he is quick as a cat, and his strength is immense; let him once get to close quarters, and get a hug at you, even though your knife arm be free, your chances are slim in coming out victor; he can ward off a blow so quick, that the motion of the huge paw can scarce be observed, and that terrible hind foot, with its powerful claws, can disembowel its assailant with one downward stroke …

Thursday, September 19. Matty Sherratt, a young fellow attached to the trains, and herding some sore backed mules, and the cattle we are bringing along for Beef by and by, came into my camp this evening from his post some 5 miles away, and says the Bears have fairly driven him out. After furnishing him another man from one of the trains as a companion, and an additional Henry Rifle & ammunition, I told him he had best return at once, and not leave the animals to be stampeded and lost, but Sherrett was unwilling to return, and told me that yesterday, while baking his bread, a large Cinnamon Bear frequently showed himself, making him feel anything but comfortable; that finally it rushed out of the timber, and made for him open-mouthed; having only his pistol handy, he thought the better part of valour under such circumstances was to take to his heels. I fancy such a move would never have saved him, and told him so; he said, he knew that too, and that had the bear not stopped short on reaching his tent, he was sure no shadow of a chance existed in getting away. Master Bruin had it appears been tempted, even while in mad wrath, by the smell of warm bread and other edibles; and coming to a sudden halt, lost no time in eating up the poor fellow's supplies. Camp kettles were turned over, and the contents quickly demolished: in fact, Bread, Cold Meat, Apples and Sugar, was cleaned out in short order. Matty had betaken himself to a small tree, and as soon as his bearship had returned thanks, and sauntered off, he lost no time in hurrying here, and reporting progress. He was about as badly frightened as he could well be. I fear I did not help him out of his difficulties much; I told him that Bruin would, like the tramp, remember the place he had fared so well at, and had such an easy victory; and that he might rest assured he would receive another visit very shortly, &c.

The Cinnamon is in my belief the worst and most dangerous of our North American Bears. The Grizzly is no climber, but a Cinnamon is; hence, once up a tree from a Grizzly, it rests with the one who can out endure the other. The man's position is certainly the most uncomfortable, but you see, if he comes down he will die of a surety. While the Grizzly has simply revenge or a desire for the destruction of a supposed enemy to gratify, let the man hold out long enough, and his bearship will find it necessary to leave and search for food. When the man comes down, hungered too, no doubt, but taking good care to go in an opposite direction to Bruin for his food, or if he has to go that way, will make a detour. But a Cinnamon is a very savage beast, and can run at a very lively rate, spite his clumsy appearance, out stripping a man two to one, and especially in the Timber, and he can climb like a cat.

I remember well, when we (the Sappers) first came out from England, we were all anxious to see Bruin in his wild state: and by our camp fires we were a brave set; this was in 1859, and it so happened, that I, together with four or five of my comrades were out in the woods, along a trail that had been made, and were probably a mile or so from camp, when somehow I got ahead of the others, and knowing none of them had fire arms, something put it into my head to try and scare them; getting off the trail therefore, I crouched down behind some underbrush, and as they came abreast of me, I growled as deep as I could, and then gave a short whining grunt; then another deep growl. It is likely they had not noted my absense, however that might be, they took the alarm, and let out towards camp at a terrific rate. I stood and laughed after they were gone, enjoying the joke immensely, and seating myself on a log by the side of the trail, I commenced filling my pipe; suddenly a cracking in the timber behind me caused me to turn, and through the thick undergrowth I could see his bearship nosing his way directly towards me, unconscious of my presence I make no doubt. Just about that time

I had no curiosity to see Bruin in his native wilds, although I had repeatedly expressed such a wish. I was off that log, and dancing along that trail at a lively rate, more frightened I dare venture than those other fellows. Just as I panted into camp I met a dozen coming out armed for a bear hunt; and instead of letting them go on a wild goose chase, and laughing in my sleeve, I joined them, but we did not get him; he heard or scented us, and made off …

Sunday, October 6. At an old camping ground of the party, and as we were tightening the ropes on the animal's packs, before crossing a deep fording place, two of the Packers who were some distance from the others, I observed were shying stones into the bushes; the dog at my heels observing them likewise tore up to the spot barking furiously. Guessing it was some animal they were throwing at, I took no further notice; but presently one of the men shouted to me to bring up my Rifle. It so happened I had not my Rifle with me, only my Revolver; I went forward however, to satisfy my curiosity, and found a more than half grown Cinnamon Bear was in the old camp, and Master Nip skipping around him at a respectful distance. Bruin had his temper pretty well aroused was evident; and as the dog kept harassing him, darting at his heels, his time was pretty well occupied. Knowing full well my Pistol was about of as much use as a boy's Pop Gun, I did not quite stomach the idea of going near him, but as mine appeared to be the only offensive weapon at hand, and fearing to be considered to have shown the white feather, I advanced, determined not to fire until close upon him, and inwardly praying he would turn and run, and I have no doubt such a move would have suited him, only for the dog's movements. After several attempts to strike Nip down, he turned his attention to me; I was now getting uncomfortably close. I encouraged Nip all I could to worry him, and that I believe, and that alone, kept him from attacking me. Opening his cavernous mouth, he advanced a few steps, and reared; but Nip was upon him from behind, and he dropped, and made for the dog, then ran off a few paces and faced and reared again as I still kept advancing, and Nip was attacking at all points at once, the bearship likewise thought as I did, and took to his heels, crashing through the thicket, with Nip closely following.

Now, I am aware the Dog could do no harm to such an animal, beyond harassing him, but he did so most effectually, and I was glad when he came trotting back, with his tongue out, and highly delighted doubtless at his success. I can't understand why the packers were without arms; it is the first and only time I ever caught them so. As a general thing, they are not happy save with a revolver slung to them. I thought bear signs were thick enough at Placid river and along Kimbasket Lake, but here, one cant go a hundred yards scarcely without seeing signs, and their droppings are everywhere. This is to be accounted for in a measure, feed having become now scarce on the steep sides of the hills, they are forced into the valley. Moose and Elk for herbage, and the tender branches; and bear for the Skunk Cabbage and berries &c. My camp is I dare say a bonanza they covet, and I am satisfied there are always some lurkers in my neighbourhood, not only by the restless movements of the dog, but I can hear them, and not unfrequently smell them during the night. When upon Skunk Cabbage, their droppings can be smelt quite a distance. The Bacon, Sugar &c are delicacies Bear are extremely fond of. I hardly dare venture to think what might be the result had I to dispense with the bright light in my tent throughout the night, with so many ursine neighbours near, and so many toothsome dainties around me.

I had forgotten to mention that I endeavoured to make a sketch of some light foliage up a gulch not far from my camp, and during a respite the rain god had given us, fortunate for me probably, I was partially hidden by low shrubs in the valley, and seated as I was upon a piece of drift timber, only my head and shoulders were visible. I had made some progress with my sketch, and was about quitting the spot, when I heard a rustling amid the foliage I had been penciling down, and so waited patiently to see what came of it. I guessed it was a bear, as I knew it was a heavy body moving about. But I got my Rifle ready, hoping it might prove to emerge an Elk or Moose. At length it did emerge, and shaped itself into the powerful form of a Grizzly—and such a monster I had never beheld, looking to me as large as an ox. He was evidently a patriarch among his savage brethren, as grizzly an old rascal as could well be imagined. The hide appeared as though it laid in flaps or plaits over his shoulders, and as he stood irresolute, looking up and down the Valley, my heart went pit a pat, for I feared every moment he would observe me, and being on the open ground, I had no friendly tree I could take shelter in. The idea of conquering such an animal with my Winchester never occurred to me, and I dare not fire; luckily it did not take him long to decide his course, which was away from my camp, and up the Valley towards the foot of the pass. I watched him leisurely shambling off, and finally had the satisfaction of seeing him turn a bend in the foot hills and disappear, a veritable Sampson.

GRIZZLY IN THE SNOW

Col. P. Robertson-Ross

Poor unsuspecting bears who encountered early travellers in the mountains were often met with a fusillade of gunfire, much of it from weapons incapable of dispatching a bear. Such was the fate of the grizzly that stumbled into the snowbound camp of Colonel P. Robertson-Ross in September 1872. As commanding officer of the Militia of Canada, Ross was on a reconnaissance trip through western Canada, and was travelling with his 16-year-old son Hugh, a Stoney Indian named Benjamin, and the veteran half-breed guide Piscan Munro, when the party was hit by an early season storm in the foothills south of Highwood River.

MONDAY, September 23. Still snowed up. No sign up to this hour (9 A.M.) of weather improving. It snowed all last night and is now steadily snowing, prospect very gloomy.

12 o'clock noon, weather has cleared up a little and we can now see some distance from our most desolate and forlorn looking little camp ...

Shortly before 1 P.M. I happened to look out of our little camp and lo I saw a large Grizzly Bear coming towards us wading through the snow. I was not more than 50 yards off. I instantly gave the alarm and got hold of Hugh's Revolver. "Benjamin" the Stoney Indian was the first man ready after myself but he spoilt the fun at this moment being frightened I suppose by firing too soon, otherwise I have no doubt the animal would have come right on our little camp which was half buried in the snow. As soon as "Benjamin" fired the Bear turned and made off. I fired three shots in succession at it with the revolver as it was making off but without effect. The snow being very deep the bear could not go fast through it, so we got our horses and accompanied by Hugh, Monroe

50

and Benjamin we followed the animal, which took refuge in a patch of bushes about 2 or 400 yards from the camp. Surrounding the bush we shouted and fired several shots in to the bushes which had the effect of bringing out the bear to the edge of the bush close to where I was with Hugh and Benjamin all sitting quietly on our horses. "Benjamin" saw the bear first and fired with his flint gun, a useless weapon, missing. I then got a fair shot at it with my Snider Carbine the animal being not more than 10 or at most 12 yards from me but much concealed in a thick bush. I felt sure my ball had struck having taken a steady aim, and the animal seemed to fall as it were, at all events, did not rush out as it seemed to be on the point of doing but disappeared. Not knowing for certain it was hit we hunted about for some time, and at last Benjamin dismounted and creeping cautiously into the bush followed by Monroe and myself he saw the bear lying dead where I had fired at it, but to make sure Monroe fired again into it, calling out to me however at the time that the animal was already dead, and so it was.

It turned out to be a very large Grizzly bear (a she bear) and is a great prize. On skinning and cutting up the animal we found my bullet in it, which had struck the bear between the shoulders and passing downward through his ribs had gone right through the heart killing the animal instantly. It was a very lucky shot and one I feel rather proud of. Hugh behaved very well indeed and does not seem the least frightened of what is considered hereabouts the most dangerous sport. Monroe and Benjamin skinned the Grizzly which I hope to preserve as a trophy, and cut up the animal for meat and we were back in camp with the work all done and at our dinner at 3 P.M. much pleased with our good fortune. Both Hugh and I were amazed at the size and strength of the Grizzly, which Monroe tells me is a fine specimen of an old Grizzly. When Benjamin fired, Monroe tried to do so also, but something went wrong with his rifle (a Sixteen Shooter) and at the critical moment it would not go off. He called out to me to lend him my revolver expecting that the bear was about to charge at us. I handed him the revolver, and then leveling my Carbine fired the shot which ended the career of poor "Bruin." Altogether I am rather a proud man today.

In the afternoon the weather cleared up and it became fine in the evening the stars came out, but oh what a wintry scene. At night "Benjamin" the Stoney treated us to the Indian Bear Song, amid the dismal howlings of which I laid down to sleep, with Hugh rolled up in a Buffalo robe alongside me.

III

WILDERNESS BEARS

Adventures in Grizzly Country

TRACKS ON THE TRAIL

Hugh E. M. Stutfield and J. Norman Collie

Hugh Stutfield and Norman Collie were British mountaineers who journeyed to the Rockies in 1898 in search of unclimbed summits in the Canadian Alps. Like many of the early visitors to the Rockies and Selkirks, they were experienced world travellers. Just as the CPR advertising had promised, they found mountains that compared quite favourably to the European Alps. But they also discovered something they'd never encountered on the trails of Switzerland—grizzly bears.

STUTFIELD, loth to quit the mountains, and wishing to see something of the Selkirks, went to Glacier House and stayed there a week. The charms of this delightful little Canadian Pacific Railway hostel and its neighbourhood have been written of at length … The hotel stands at the narrow entrance of a curious deep bay in the hills; and few more striking effects can be seen anywhere than when, as the train emerges from the long dark snow-sheds—or, if the traveller is east-bound, after creeping round those wonderful loops in the line, and over the spider-legged trestle-bridges—the Great Glacier bursts into view, gleaming white amid the pines, with the splendid crags of Mount Sir Donald frowning down upon you.

When Stutfield arrived, however, he found other and more pressing matters than the scenery to occupy his attention. The tracks of an enormous grizzly and her two cubs had just been discovered on the trail leading to the Asulkan Glacier, less than an hour's walk from the hotel. They had been made that morning or during the night, and were of quite remarkable size. One reads in the older travel-books of grizzlies' foot-prints almost as long as a man's fore-arm; and the comparison is hardly an exaggerated one. We carefully measured the marks with a piece of string, which unfortunately got lost; but they were certainly well over a foot in length, and broad in proportion. Much more extraordinary than their mere size, however, was the juxtaposition, in a patch of soft mud, of two tracks that offered a most curious contrast. Side by side, only a few inches apart, were the huge grizzly's spoor and the tiny imprint of a lady's smart Parisian shoe! The wearer of the shoe, a lady who is a frequent visitor at the Glacier House, had passed along the trail the preceding afternoon on a walk through the valley, and *ursus horribilis* must have followed a few hours later.

We followed the tracks some way down the banks of the stream, until we lost them in the forest. Three days were spent in a hunt after the grizzly, fish and meat being hung on the trees for bait, but not a sign of it could be discovered. A couple of days later a very large bear, measuring nine feet from snout to tail, was shot with her two cubs near Rogers' Pass, three miles up the railway; and, as the tracks we had seen headed in that direction, this was no doubt the same beast. Bears, black, brown, and grizzly, are by no means uncommon in the Selkirks; but hunting for them in those vast, dense, and trackless forests is like looking for the proverbial needle in a haystack. The Canadian Pacific Railway section men often see them crossing the railway; and in winter they are occasionally shot from the windows of the hotel. They told us at Glacier of a funny adventure which befell two girls belonging to a party of "Christian Adventurers" who were making a tour through the country. Being greatly daring spirits, they had borrowed ice-axes from the hotel and gone for a walk alone up the Illecillewaet ice-fall. Descending towards evening, they were about to leave the glacier by the only feasible way off the ice, when, to their horror, they saw an old she-grizzly and her cub on the moraine just in front of them. Not daring to advance, they remained on the glacier till near midnight, when they were rescued by a search-party from the hotel. The ferocity of grizzly bears in these later days is nothing like what is represented in the older books on Rocky Mountain sport. Experience, probably, has taught them that their teeth and claws are no match for modern repeating rifles. Unless surprised at close quarters with their cubs, or when feeding on a carcase, they will very seldom attack a man: and in the Yellowstone Park, where

Stutfield saw them in considerable numbers, they appear to be more shy even than the deer, and vanish the moment they catch sight of their human foes.

MY GRIZZLY-BEAR DAY

William T. Hornaday

William Temple Hornaday was Director of the New York Zoological Park when he came to the Canadian Rockies in 1905 to collect specimens of mountain goat and sheep. But his guide Charlie Smith managed to lure him away from the focus of his expedition long enough to go in search of grizzly bear. In the end, the renowned conservationist found himself torn between simply observing this symbol of the North American wilderness or bagging it as a trophy to satisfy his guide.

WHEN one can start out from camp, and in a walk of two hours find at least a dozen rubbing-trees of grizzly bears, each one with bear hair clinging to its bark, then may one say, "This is bear country!" That was what we found in the green timber of Avalanche Valley, between our camp and Roth Mountain, six miles below. All the rubbing-trees we saw were from eight to twelve inches in diameter, as if small ones had been specially chosen. I suppose this is because there are no large spur roots to interfere with the standing bear; besides which, a small tree offers a sharper edge.

On those trees we saw where several of the rubbing bears had bitten the trunk, high up, tearing the bark open crosswise. We also found, on some, raking claw-marks across the bark. Charlie Smith said that the tooth-marks are always made by grizzlies and the claw-marks by black bears.

As before remarked, Mr. Phillips and Charlie Smith were very desirous that I should find and kill a grizzly, but for several reasons I had little hope that it would come to pass. September is not a good month in which to find a bear of any species on those summits; nor is a short hunting-trip conducive to the development of bear-episodes, anywhere. In spite of Charlie's hopefulness, I did not take the prospect seriously, even though in the Michel store Mack had called for twine with which to stretch bear-hides! But in bear-hunting, "it is better to be born lucky than rich."

When Charlie came in on the evening of the 19th of September and reported a bear at the carcass of my first goat, it really seemed time to hope for at least a distant view of Old Ephraim. Believing that one good way to reveal certain phases of wild-animal life is in showing how animals are actually found in their haunts, I am tempted to set forth a statement of the events of September 20th. It may be that others wonder, as I often have, just how it *feels* to hunt a grizzly bear—the most dangerous American animal—and find him, at timberline. The really bold hunters may scoff at the courage and ferocity of the grizzly as he is to-day; but Charlie Smith openly declares that the one particular thing which he never does, and never will do, is to fire his last cartridge when away from camp.

It was the third day of Mr. Phillips's hunt for mountain sheep, and he was still absent. Charlie and I took two saddle-horses and set out before sunrise, intending to visit all the goat carcasses before returning. We pushed briskly up to the head of Avalanche Creek, climbed to the top of the pass, then dropped down into the basin on the north. I dreaded a long climb on foot from that point up to our old camp on Goat Pass, but was happily disappointed. Thanks to the good engineering of some Indian trail-maker, the trail led from the head of the basin, on an easy gradient, up through the green timber of the mountain side, quite to our old camp.

We found fresh grizzly-bear tracks within fifty feet of the ashes of our camp-fire; but our goat skins in the big spruce, and our cache of provisions near it, had not been touched ...

With only a few minutes delay, we mounted once more and rode on northward toward the scene of the first goat-kill. As we rode up the ridge of Bald Mountain, a biting cold wind, blowing sixty miles an hour, struck us with its full force. It went through our clothing like cold water, and penetrated to the marrow in our bones. At one point it seemed determined to blow the hair off Kaiser's back. While struggling to hold myself together, I saw the dog suddenly whirl head on to the fierce blast, crouch low, and fiercely grip the turf with his claws, to keep from being blown away. It was all that our horses could do to hold a straight course, and keep from drifting down to the very edge of the precipice that yawned only twenty-five feet to leeward. We were glad to get under the lee of Bald Mountain, where the fierce blast that concentrated on that bleak pass could not strike us with its full force.

At last we reached the lake we named in honor of Kaiser. Dismounting in a grassy hollow that was sheltered from the wind, we quickly stripped the saddles from our horses and picketed the animals so that they could graze. Then, catching up our rifles, cameras, and a very slim parcel of luncheon, we set out past the lake for the ridge that rises beyond it.

The timber on the ridge was very thin, and we could see through it for a hundred yards or more. As we climbed, we looked sharply all about, for it seemed very probable that a grizzly might be lying beside a log in the fitful sunshine that struck the southern face of the hill. Of course, as prudent hunters, we were prepared to see a grizzly that was above us, and big, and dangerous,—three conditions that guarantee an interesting session whenever they come together ...

We reached the crest of the ridge, without having seen a bear, and with the utmost caution stalked on down the northern side, toward the spot where the two goat carcasses lay on the slide-rock. The noise we made was reduced to an irreducible minimum.

We trod and straddled like men burglarizing Nature's sky-parlor. We broke no dead twigs, we scraped against no dead branches, we slid over no fallen logs. Step by step we stole down the hillside, as cautiously as if we had known that a bear was really at the foot of it. At no time would it have surprised us to have seen Old Ephraim spring up from behind a bush or fallen log, within twenty feet of us.

At last the gray slide-rock began to rise into view. At last we paused, breathing softly and seldom, behind a little clump of spruces. Charlie, who was a step in advance, stretched his neck to its limit, and looked on beyond the edge of the hill, to the very spot where lay the remains of my first mountain goat. My view was cut off by green branches and Charlie.

He turned to me, and whispered in a perfectly colorless way, "He's lying right on the carcass!"

"What? Do you mean to say that a *bear* is *really there?*" I asked, in astonishment.

"Yes! Stand here, and you can see him,—just over the edge."

I stepped forward and looked. Far down, fully one hundred and fifty yards from where we were, there lay a silvery-gray animal, head up, front paws outstretched. It was indeed a silver-tip; but it looked awfully small and far away. He was out on the clean, light-gray stipple of slide-rock, beside the scanty remains of my goat.

Even as I took my first look, the animal rose on his haunches, and for a moment looked intently toward the north, away from us. The wind waved his long hair, one wave after another. It was a fine chance for a line shot at the spinal column; and at once I made ready to fire.

"Do you think you can kill him from *here?*" asked Charlie, anxiously. "You can get nearer to him if you like."

"Yes; I think I can hit him from here all right." (I had carefully fixed the sights of my rifle, several days previously.)

"Well, if you don't hit him, I'll kick you down this ridge!" said Charlie, solemn as a church owl, with an on-your-head-be-it air. To me, it was clearly a moment of great peril.

I greatly desired to watch that animal for half an hour; but when a bear-hunter finds a grizzly bear, the thing for him to do is to kill it first, and watch afterward. I realized that no amount of bear observations ever could explain to John Phillips the loss of that bear.

As I raised my .303 Savage, the grizzly rose in a business-like way, and started to walk up the slide-rock, due south, and a little quartering from us. This was not half so good for me as when he was sitting down. Aiming to hit his heart and lungs, close behind his foreleg, and allowing a foot for his walking, I let go.

A second or two after the "whang" the bear reared slightly, and sharply wheeled toward his right, away from us; and just then Charlie's rifle roared,—close beside my ear! Without losing an instant, the grizzly started on a mad gallop, down the slide-rock and down the canyon, running squarely across our front.

"Heavens!" I thought, aghast. *"Have I missed him?"*

Quickly I threw in another cartridge, and fired again; and "whang" went Charlie, as before. The bear fairly flew, reaching far out with its front feet, its long hair rolling in great waves from head to tail. Even at that distance, its silver-tipped fur proclaimed the species.

Bushes now hid my view, and I ran down a few yards, to get a fair show. At last my chance came. As the bear raced across an opening in my view, I aimed three feet ahead of his nose, and fired my third shot.

Instantly the animal pitched forward on his head, like a stricken rabbit, and lay very still.

"Ye fetched him that time!" yelled Charlie, triumphantly. "He's down! He's down! Go for him, Kaiser! Go for him!"

The dog was ready to burst with superheated eagerness. With two or three whining yelps he dashed away down the ridge, and out of sight. By this time Charlie was well below me, and I ran down to where he stood, beaming up.

"You've fixed him, Director! He's down for keeps."

"Where is he?"

"Lying right on that patch of yellow grass, and dead as a wedge. *Shake!*"

TESTING A THEORY

R. M. Patterson

Patterson's Buffalo Head Ranch was located on the Highwood River in Alberta's rolling foothills country. On one of his many horseback excursions during the 1930s, he led a young lady from Toronto on an exciting adventure into the high, open country west of the ranch.

ABOUT seven miles from home the trail came out of a belt of pines on to a very steep, open, bunch-grass hillside. We were entering the upper part of Bull Creek valley; and this bit of country was, and still is, a living memorial of what the foothills must have been before the white man came, measuring and parcelling, ploughing up, overgrazing with his cattle and horses. The bunch-grass grew there as it had always grown, with its roots protected from sun and frost by thick cushions of its own old growth. In summertime it bent before the onrush of the wind like a field of waving grain; its swaying seed heads made a rippling sea of silver light, splashed with the flaring colour of the summer flowers. In the fall the bunch-grass cured and ripened. Deer and elk passed by, and perhaps some wandering, pioneering cow and calf. But no herd came this way to break the quiet of this lonely valley. Then, through the lazy, slumbrous days of Indian summer, the grass hillsides would lie pale gold under the low autumn sun, shining with a light of their own against the dark rocks and the black woods of alpine firs, waiting ...

But this was May, and last year's grass lay dun-coloured and flattened by the winter snows. In this carpet of old grass the crocuses were flowering and the young green blades were poking through. The blue, snow-streaked summit of the Holy Cross showed to the westward through the pass, and down the valley sang the everlasting westwind.

In the sun-warmed watercourses that wrinkled this hillside an early growth always started up, and the tender, juicy shoots of certain plants were already showing. One of these favoured spots lay about three hundred yards ahead of us and there was something very odd protruding from it—a pale-coloured, roundish shape through the edges of which the afternoon sun made a halo of light. I watched it for a minute or so. It was very busy, whatever it was, and it was scarcely moving. Then I saw—and I turned in my saddle and pointed: "Look, Nancy—a grizzly!"

"No!" she said, leaning forward. "Oh, where? Show me at once! Can we get closer?" Her eyes were shining with excitement.

"I think we can," I said, and we moved forward. The wind blew in our faces, straight from the grizzly to us, and, what with the rush and the roaring of it and the tumult of Bull Creek away down below, one could speak in an ordinary quiet voice without disturbing the bear. And the grizzly was feeding away from us into the wind; the round thing, which was all that I had so far seen of him, was a bit of his rump sticking up over the lip of the little coulee that he was grubbing in.

The trail was nothing but an old game trail, about a foot or eighteen inches wide. High above us on our right there was a belt of pines. Deep down on our left Bull Creek fought its noisy way through old snowdrifts and a tangle of twisted poplar and willow. It was a case of either up the trail or down the trail—there was no other place to run to if anything went wrong. And the outfit consisted of one optimistic rancher, one overloaded packhorse running loose, and one girl from Toronto, brimful of confidence (in what? I have often wondered) and breathless with excitement.

I had been reading Bryan Williams' book, *Game Trails in British Columbia*. Bryan Williams had been a guide in the Kootenays and in the Cassiar, then, for thirteen years, head of the B.C. Provincial Game Department. If he didn't know what he was talking about, then who did? In his book Williams gives it as his opinion that a grizzly, when startled, will run in whatever direction he happens to be facing at that moment. Most of the "charges" attributed to these bears, Williams says, are due to the fact that, when the shot is fired or the grizzly is otherwise alarmed, he takes immediate steps to get away from trouble—and very often the quickest way to do that is to follow his nose and not waste time looking around. And sometimes his nose happens to be pointing towards the hunter ...

This grizzly had his back to us and was fully occupied with his spring salad. I had full confidence in Bryan Williams' well-argued theory: never would there be a better chance of putting it to the test. And so we rode quietly up the trail.

There must be some minor deity whose special duty it is to protect the foolhardy, for, without any exaggeration, we rode to within twenty-five yards of that grizzly. I have often passed that spot since then and never without marvelling at the few short paces we left between ourselves and that bunch of living dynamite. It was not my old friend, the red-legged grizzly whom I often saw here. This bear was of one uniform colour, almost sandy with a touch of grey. He was very big and the wind was rippling his pale fur and sending small shadows chasing through it. He was grubbing away with claws and teeth in the soft earth, pursuing his tender mushy plants, and he was completely absorbed in his quest.

I turned round to look at Nancy. She was leaning forward in her saddle fascinated, absolutely entranced. The curious thing is that the sense of fear seemed to be absent that afternoon. The horses, too, were not alarmed; they were watching the bear quite quietly.

"What do we do now?" Nancy said, raising her voice just enough to cope with the wind.

The thing had gone far enough. "We speak to him," I said; and I turned and shouted, putting my trust in Bryan Williams: "Hullo, Bear!" It wasn't a particularly bright remark, but it worked like a charm. Without pausing to look behind, the grizzly lit out of there as if the devil was after him—straight the way he was heading, which was up and across the hill. The speed at which he moved was something of an eye-opener when seen from so close. He never stopped or looked behind him till he reached the edge of the pines above us; then he turned round, raised up on his hind legs to his full height, lifted his paws and let a roar out of him that could be heard by us down on the trail, even with that wind blowing.

"What do we do *now?*" Nancy asked.

"We get out of here quick," I told her, "and let's hope he isn't a she with some cubs somewhere up the trail." And we rode on up the valley, not slowly but not without dignity.

THE AGONY
OF WARDEN MCDONALD

Sid Marty

O N a dark night, it's best to rely on your nose when you walk out to check your horses, not just your eyes. A grizzly on all fours may look like a horse when there are only the stars for lamps.

An old-time Jasper warden, Ed McDonald, took the situation to its logical, if frightening, conclusion, in a high, lonesome valley one night. He went out in the dark to get his horses in for an early start the next day and walked toward what he thought was a horse cropping grass a few yards away. "Ho, pony," Ed said softly, so as not to spook the horse by surprising it, "easy now, big fellah." He stepped up to its shoulder, and reached out with the halter but froze when he felt long, shaggy fur instead of horsehide. The bear snarled once and, chopping its jaws together with a sound like a steel box closing in an empty room, it moved quickly away to find a less crowded place to feed, leaving Ed shivering with the halter still held in his outstretched hand. If Ed laughed over that one, he must have waited until he got down to the old log shack in Jasper, where, in those days, the wardens used to rendezvous to drink whiskey and swap stories. The shack is gone now but the stories live on.

For most of Ed's career, he had the Rocky River district which stretched from the Athabasca River, up the Rocky, and along the east park boundary to the limits of the Brazeau district at Southesk Pass. The area was, and still is, some of the last unruined wilderness to be found south of the Northwest Territories. It's a land of narrow valleys, bisected by swift-flowing streams like the Rocky, Restless, and Medicine

Tent Rivers. But it isn't the fast water and big lonely mountains staring down that make it wild, it's the track of the grizzly to be found in the high passes and in the tributary valleys of the Rocky River. There were many bears in the district back then, and Ed came and went among them without giving it much thought.

Having once tried to halter old humpback, and having lived to tell the tale, Ed lost his fear of the bear. Once, Ed's doughtiness, and a couple of machinegun bullets he'd been carrying in his leg since the First World War, combined in an accident that nearly cost him his life.

One day in June of 1937, Ed was returning to his line cabin on the Medicine Tent River after a day spent siwashing up to the head of a nearby creek. It was part of the warden's job then to explore and map every brook in his district so as to monitor its potential for fire protection and to discover what big game animals ranged its upper slopes and at what time of year. Ed couldn't stand not knowing about every creek, valley, and meadow in his district. An unknown place pricked at his peace of mind like a sliver under a fingernail; he couldn't sit still until he had probed it out completely.

It had been a long day. Ed's fifty-seven winters combined with the warm sun of late afternoon weighed heavily on his eyelids, so he drowsed in the saddle, riding with a slack rein. Sometimes he loosed his right leg from the stirrup and let it trail free, because the chunks of steel-jacketed lead the Army doctors had overlooked pinched the nerves at times, making it painful to bend his knee. Now and again the horse, sensing that its rider was dozing off, would stoop to steal a mouthful of grass along the way but mostly it stepped along quick enough, headed for the cabin and a bait of oats.

Ed's dog Willie, a six-month-old collie pup, ran along under the stirrup. Ed trusted the horse. It was a seasoned animal that knew the country well and knew the dangers too. They had seen a silvertip earlier that day, feeding on the broad leaves of cow parsnip at the edge of a small meadow near the trail, but Ed had passed it off as just another grizzly. The horse had never run from a bear before. This time, though, it must have come on to the bear sign too fast, or perhaps the wind changed suddenly and the horse got too much bear stink all at once, because it suddenly shied violently, and Ed, not having a good seat, with one leg out of the stirrup, found himself flying off before he could gather rein. He lighted on his back right on a dead tree that lay beside the trail. Something gave with a snap that made him yell with agony and, winded, he lay still, wondering what had hit him. Before he could move, the horse came by him, bucking, and kicked him hard on the hip bone. Still unaware of how badly he was hurt, in the numbness that sometimes follows a serious injury, Ed tried to get up but found he could not stand. His pelvis was broken.

Old Ed had hit the jackpot and he knew it. He eased himself over on his stomach and felt his mind clouding with a pain that smoked along his hips and burned along the fuse of every nerve. He was in need of a doctor and a hospital but the nearest medical help was forty-two miles away. Considering the shape he was in, it may as well have been on the moon and he knew that a week might easily go by before anyone came looking for him. It had been a warm spring and the rivers were beginning to flood with runoff. In Jasper, they might figure a section of phone line had been washed out and they would allow him enough time to fix it, maybe five days, before they got worried and sent somebody looking for him. That's what had happened to Goodair. Ed's eyes focused on the wire that waved slightly in the breeze, twenty feet above him. He wished he had had his field-set with him but it was back in the cabin, only half a mile away. Surely he could make it half a mile, such a short distance. He tried to get up again but it was as if, in order to stand, he had to slide his groin along the sharp edge of a knife. He fell back, moaning with shock.

The horse had settled down and was feeding on the trail behind him. It would have to pass close to him to get up to the cabin where the pack ponies were picketed in the meadow. He saw the shape of an eleven-inch-long grizzly track, pressed into the wet earth between his hands, the track twice as big as his own palm prints, and he then knew what had frightened his horse. A twig snapped behind him and he felt the warm breath of an animal on the back of his neck. He yelled with fear and rolled over to meet it, reaching for his belt knife. There was the dog, backing away from him, terrified.

Calling the dog to him, he lay still, fighting the pain, until the horse drew near and the reins flicked over his arm. While the horse stood patiently, Ed hauled himself up on the stirrup leathers until he was nearly standing. Though he tried repeatedly, he could not get into the saddle. At length, he pulled out the cinch knot, dropped the saddle and blanket to the ground, pulled off the bridle, and with one hand on a nearby spruce lowered himself to the ground where he lay, soaking wet with sweat from the pain of the wasted effort. He wrapped himself in the saddle blankets, and covered himself with his slicker, not having the strength to crawl around gathering wood for a fire. The dog lay down with him, offering its loyalty and the meagre warmth of its body. The dog growled steadily at something in the woods by the trail that Ed didn't want to see or think about, though he knew it was the bear.

Two days passed while Ed lay under a spruce tree, hoping that he would improve enough to be able to move, or that help would come from Jasper. On the evening of the second day, the weather changed, and a light rain fell on the two miserable figures lying under a spruce tree. With the cold of evening, the rain turned to snow. During the night the bear came closer but the dog never left Ed's side to provoke the grizzly into attacking. In the morning the whiskey-jacks looked down on a circle of bear tracks printed in the snow around the two huddled figures blanketed in white. From time to time, the dog lifted its head from Ed's shoulder and growled at the form that moved slowly through the thickets nearby, feeding on willow shoots and the green grass that poked through the spring snow.

Later in the day, the sun stirred Ed awake and it came to him that he would die where he lay, if he didn't try to move. He began to move with the slow reluctance of a creature wrested from hibernation. He blinked at the snow, forgetting where he was, then felt pain stirring in his body and he remembered the accident. Heat and cold played with his nerves; his tongue was swollen with thirst, lying in his mouth like a dead mouse, and the sound of his voice made the dog cringe.

The stiffness in his hips was the first paralyzing rigour of death and his abdomen was abnormally swollen and discoloured with infection from the damaged tissues inside. Fever made him sweat and shiver by turns. How would he find the strength to move? Then he heard the sound of the creek, its murmur amplified by the delirium of his thirst. He scooped some fast-melting snow into his mouth and the slight taste of water goaded him to try. He looped the blankets over his back, knowing that he would die of exposure without them, and began to crawl. He crawled, propped on his elbows, with the dog running up to lick his face now and then, trying to join in the game.

His mind could no longer deal with the distance there was to the cabin, so, like a crafty strategist, he promised himself he would only go as far as the creek. The dog ran to the creek occasionally through the day for a drink, returning with its fur wet from wading in the sweet water.

In the late afternoon, a roaring began in his ears. He stopped, but the roaring went on, so he kept going; but the roaring grew louder. He held his hands to his ears and yelled to drown it out. When he looked down, there was the creek a few feet away. He slid into it belly first, breathing in the water, letting it wash over his burning head, then he forced himself to wait, to drink the ice cold element in slowly, filling his inflamed stomach a little at a time. Then he crawled across the shallow ford, hauling himself up on tree roots, and laid his burning head on the cool, damp earth. He slept.

It was near dawn when Ed woke to the low, steady growl of the dog which strained against him, frightened. He looked around and saw two shapes standing in the morning mist of the creek a few yards away. He opened his mouth to speak and, hearing a low, moaning cry, he was unsure whether it was his own voice or a stranger's. Then, the two figures dropped to all fours with a splash and he heard them coming up the bank through the alder bush on either side of him and he heard the rattle of their long claws on the stones. He felt the thin earth trembling under his back as they passed him and went up the trail. The bear had brought a friend.

All that day the bears walked beside him in the thickets on either side of the trail, while the dog circled him, bristling and growling as he crawled. Their interest kept him going, for he knew they wouldn't bother him until he gave up completely. Then they would drag his corpse off the trail by the scruff of the neck, cache him under a pile of debris, until he got ripe enough to stink, before they fed on him. At dark, he heard the horse whinnying at the cabin and knew he was close. Sometime after that the bears left him and the only sound was his own harsh breath and his body dragging along the ground. By dawn, he reached the clearing and the cabin. The horses winded him first. Snorting and whinnying with hunger, they watched him crawl into the yard and they pawed the earth with impatience, having eaten the grass down to the roots for twenty-yard circles around their picket pins.

Ed ignored them, concentrating on the few yards of ground he had yet to win. The thought that the telephone might not be working had been in the back of Ed's head for four days. He had kept the idea at bay, but now it suddenly pushed against his will with a clarity that made him stop and cry out. He shook his head as if to clear the notion away by a physical effort, and kept going. All night, he had been thinking about the cabin, the food and the dry blankets, and about the telephone on the wall, high on the wall. He inched his way to the cabin door where he stopped and picked up a stick, using it to open the latch above him. The door creaked open; light poured in through the opening, glinting on the shiny metal of the telephone.

The set was on the end wall, five feet off the floor, looming overhead with the metal crank on the side that he must reach somehow to call for help. Praying that someone might already be talking on the party line, he used a broom to knock the receiver off the hook. It dangled on its long cord just over his head and, miraculously, there was Charlie Matheson's voice.

Unable to speak at first, Ed gathered his strength to shout, "Charlie. It's Ed McDonald. I'm hurt. I'm hurt real bad."

A pause, then, "Ed! I hear you, Ed. Hang on! I'll get help to you right away!"

Ed watched the black receiver swinging over his head from its cord; he could hear the voices talking faintly above him. They had heard him, they were coming to help.

He got a can of fruit and a bottle of overproof rum from the cupboard under the phone, hacked open the can with his belt knife and drank the sugary syrup, washing it down with a jolt of rum.

What Ed did next may leave the reader incredulous, but the facts are a matter of record, and they show the true mettle of Ed McDonald. He knew that his horses were starving, so he dragged himself out to the darkening meadow, slashed their picket ropes and crawled back to the cabin where he wrapped himself in the blankets and lay there nursing the bottle of pain killer.

In Jasper, a rescue party was organized. Charlie Matheson was ordered to form a party with two local men, Joe Weiss and Roy Knutson. Frank Wells was dispatched from Jasper with Dan Blacklock and Bruce Otto, two mountain men noted for their strength and stamina, and Dr. Donovan Ross. They had a thirty-mile ride to make at night, so they pressed on through the blackness. Frank said Ed McDonald was more dead than alive when they got there, sometime after midnight; the outside of his stomach was black, green, and yellow, and his urine was nearly straight blood. The doctor fixed him up as best he could, before tending to his own injuries—saddle sores.

They laid over a day, building up Ed's strength for the journey while the men built a travois to sling between two horses in Indian file. Ed started to feel better, raising hell with the boys for putting his pots in the wrong cupboard and not washing his cups thoroughly. At 8:00 the next morning they wrapped him in blankets and canvas and loaded him in the travois. They said Old Ed knew where he was the whole trip, although his face was covered by the canvas to keep out the rain. He could tell where they were by the sound of the horses' feet and kept himself occupied telling the men to watch for a fork in the trail they were coming to or giving them hell for trying to sneak by his drift fences without putting the bars up.

The travois was too long to go around some of the corners. They would have to stop, untie the poles from the rear horse, and carry the travois on one man's shoulders, a feat that only strong men and expert horsemen could accomplish because, with a broken pelvis the slightest motion can cause the victim excruciating pain. After what Ed had suffered, it was miraculous that he survived the thirty miles in the travois. At Medicine Lake, they transferred him to a boat which took him to the end of the lake where an ambulance waited to drive him to the hospital.

Old Ed recovered and he wardened many years after the accident. The story got into the press about Ed sleeping with the grizzly bears and he got letters from all over North America, full of the wildest speculation about the savagery of the bear. I think, in the end, the letters wound up making Ed a little owly on the subject because, afterwards, whenever anybody talked about how vicious the bear could be, he would say, "Hell, don't tell me they'll slap you down and eat you up. They could have had me and my dog for supper four nights running and they passed us up."

This casual dismissal of bad luck by a man who had nearly died because of one mistake on his part, was typical of the old-time wardens. Ed McDonald died at ninety-three in an old folks' home, although by all rights he should have died the night he tried to halter the grizzly bear or the day he fell asleep on his horse.

STOPPIN' FOR A SMOKE

Frank Goble

*In the spring of 1938, trappers Frank Goble, Levi Ashman, and Charlie Wise
headed back over the Great Divide from their line cabin on the headwaters of
British Columbia's Akamina-Kishenena Valley to their homes at Waterton
Lakes, Alberta.*

BY the time we'd eaten breakfast and had given the cabin sort
of a half-hearted clean-up it was full daylight. We left shortly
after sun-up, with the walking good on the hard snow and
the air fresh and crisp. As we came down the Alberta side of
the pass we met another early morning traveller coming up the trail, a
big old male grizzly, a dark reddish brown in colour, with long silver
guard hairs on his back and along his sides and with a ruff of longer fur
around his neck.

When the bear saw us coming towards him he stood up on his hind
legs for a better look and apparently not liking what he saw and smelled
he began rumbling in his throat, snapping his teeth together and shaking
his head from side to side in warning. I was in the lead and I stopped to
look him over not knowing what the big son-of-a-gun was going to do.
Charlie, who was behind me, said: "My Gawd, ain't he purty! Must be a
old feller fer t' be dat Jeezely big."

We stood there in the early morning sunlight at a distance of about
60 feet, watching each other. Levi sat down at the side of the trail and
built himself a smoke, lit it up and began puffing away at the cigarette.
Charlie looked at Levi, said to me: "Wal, kid, we-uns might jist as well
hev uh rest too whils't Levi smokes dat jeezely cigarette."

We took off our packs, dropped them to the snow, sat on them while
we watched the bear. The grizzly, seeing that we weren't going to get

out of his way, must have decided he needed a rest too because he lowered himself to all four feet, took a couple of tentative steps towards us, then when we showed no sign of moving, he too sat down in the snow, still rumbling away at us, occasionally wagging his head from side to side and snapping his teeth together.

Levi, enjoying his smoke, looked at the bear and laughed: "Well, Wise, bet this's the first time 'oo an' Fronk has sat on the side o' uh mountain with a bear that wasn't dead."

"Yeah, dat's so. Holy Gawd, ain't he uh purty Jeezely son-uv-uh-bitch! If'n we-uns wuzn't in d' Park an' if'n I-uns hed muh rifle dat w'ud be uh daid bear. Shore nice fer t' see one like dat ain't it! Tain't Jeezely often uh man hez uh chance fer t' git dis close't t' one. Mos' gen'rlly dey's on d' Jeezely run."

Levi finished his smoke: "Let's git goin'. I'm purty thirsty, ain't had no beer since New Years. If we kin git intuh Waterton early 'nough, maybe we kin ketch uh rid intuh Lethbridge today."

I was more interested in watching the grizzly than making an early appearance in Waterton, never having seen a grizzly quite that close before, and I wasn't ready to leave just yet: "Aw, there's no hurry. Let's sit here and watch him for a while. Sure wish I had some film for the camera."

The grizzly stretched out on his belly in the snow, his hind legs doubled up one on each side of his body, front legs stretched out before him, his chin laying flat on his paws, his eyes watching the three of us, an occasional low rumble coming from his chest when one of us spoke.

In and around Waterton townsite where I had lived since I was eleven years old, a good part of the local black bear population, in the spring, summer and fall, lived mainly on the garbage cans in the townsite and we thought no more of seeing a black bear than we did of seeing one of the local dogs. Sometimes a dozen or more of the blacks could be seen at one time in the evening around the townsite or at the garbage dump. However, grizzlies were much more wary than the blacks, and were seldom seen.

Levi pulled the makings out of his shirt pocket, rolled another cigarette and fired it up; Charlie decorated the clean snow in front of him with a stream of 'snoose juice,' rolled the quid of snuff back into place behind his upper lip: "Wal, kid, if'n you-uns ever hez t' git chewed up by uh Jeezely b'ar, make it uh grizzly like dat one. Uh grizzly, he-uns'll most likely jest take uh coupl'a bites an' leave but uh black bear now, he-uns'll mebbe stay right dere an' keep on chewin' til'st you-uns air daid!"

The grizzly closed his eyes, appeared to be asleep; Charlie laughed: "Look at dat Jeezely ol' son-uv-uh-gun! Ain't worried 'bout we-uns a'tall! Mus' know we-uns ain't got no rifle fer t' shoot him wid."

The bear opened his eyes, looked towards us, tipped his ears forward as if listening to what we were saying.

"You ever had trouble with a bear?"

"Naw. Never did. I-uns hev shot lots o' d' Jeezely t'ings, blacks an' grizzlies bot'. Hardest t'ing 'bout shootin' uh Grizzly is gittin' close 'nough fer uh shot. Feller down 'crost d' Line gits chewed up by uh grizzly coupl'a y'ars ago; wuz uh sow wid uh cub; dey-uns'll come fer yuh sometimes. Hed jist one come fer me, long time ago. Shot it.

"Mos'ly greenhorns whut gits in trouble wid bears, specially d' Jeezely blacks. Heered tell one time o' uh feller gittin' hisself kilt by uh black over in Idyho. B'ar stayed right dere, kep' on eatin'."

"Well, Slim was eaten by a grizzly."

"Yeah. Dat wuz diffrunt d'ough. He-uns shot hisself by accident; wuz bleedin' purty bad afore d' b'ar come. B'ar smelled d' fresh blood. Wuz mos' likely uh real ol' bear whut cud'n't hunt too good no more. Shore left big tracks, must'a bin a' old feller."

Levi wasn't interested in bears, his mind was on his thirst and all the good beer waiting for him in the city of Lethbridge. He stood up, picked up his pack, put it on: "C'mon you guys; let's git goin'."

Charlie and I got to our feet, threw on our packs. The bear sat up, looked towards us, raised up onto all four feet, whu-u-u-uffed a couple of times, wagged his big head, stood there in the trail ahead of us. Charlie said to me, me being in the lead: "Wal, kid, walk right at dat Jeezely big feller. He-uns'll git out'n d' way!"

Right at that particular moment in my life I could think of several far-away locations where I would rather have been and there were many things I would rather have done than "walk right at dat Jeezely big feller"; that bear was a whole lot bigger than I was and those long sharp claws on his front paws, together with the mouthful of white teeth that he showed when he "whu-u-u-uffed" were sort of intimidating; however, I decided I was not going to let those two old-timers know that I had considerable misgivings about walking "right at dat big feller" so I did; I "walked right at dat Jeezely big feller" standing there in the trail ahead of us although I will have to admit I didn't take very big steps and I was sort of ready to drop my pack to the snow and take off on the run for the nearest tree if the bear decided he was going to 'walk right at us.' However, after some rumbling and grumbling and snapping of his jaws together and blowing as we kept coming at him he moved off the trail, walking with a dignified, stiff-legged gait, in no hurry to get out of our way; picking each foot up and placing the paw ahead on the crusted snow in a deliberate fashion, giving it a little circular twist from side to side in the snow as he put it down, wagging his big head back and forth and growling deep in his chest as if he were talking to us and saying: "don't you fellers get the idea that I'm scared of you because I'm not, I don't give a damn about you guys I just don't want any trouble."

I didn't push him at all, figuring if he were moving out of the way that was fine with me and he could take all the time he wanted provided he kept on going in the direction in which he was headed which was off the trail and into the scattered trees up above. We passed him at a distance of about forty or fifty feet and as we passed below he stopped moving ahead, just stood there broadside to us swinging his head around to watch, about one good jump away from the three of us and I got my legs moving faster than they had been moving, anxious to get some distance between us in case he changed his mind and decided to make an investigation at close range. However he was a good bear and stayed where he was. We went on down the trail following the line of tracks he had made on his way up. I stepped into one of his paw prints, a print of one of his hind feet, and could see bear track all around my boot, which was a size 11. He was a big bear.

We stopped about a hundred yards down the trail, at the turn above the lower bridge, wanting to see what the bear would do. Looking back, we saw him come down out of the trees and move slowly up the trail to where we had been sitting. Here he sniffed at the marks left in the snow by our packs, licked at the patch of snow that had been stained yellow by Charlie's snoose 'juice,' took a swipe at the stain with his paw sending a chunk of snow sailing off into the trees below, raised up on his hind legs and looked towards us, dropped down again and walked slowly away, his big hind end rolling from side to side as his pigeon-toed ambling gait took him out of sight around the first bend in the trail, on his way through the Akamina Pass and into British Columbia, probably to his summer range in the Akamina-Kishinena Valley watershed area.

A NOCTURNAL VISIT

C.E. Millar

*Packer-cowboy poet Charles Millar was inspired to write the following verse
after a return raid on Assiniboine Lodge by a hungry grizzly bear during the
summer of 1940. Lodge owner Erling Strom and a young Norwegian employee,
Ottar Malm, are the poem's protagonists.*

A grizzly bear, one night did fare
On butter, lard and meat;
It was so good, he thought he would
This luscious feast repeat.

He waddled up again to sup
On taste-sensations rare;
When Erling 'rose, without much clothes
And saw this grizzly bear.

He grabbed his gun and on the run
He shoved the safety catch!
"The bear!" called he, "Come, Malm, with me
And we will shoot the wretch!"

So Ottar tore across the floor
With youthful might and main;
His bare legs flashed, so swift he dashed
Up to the window pane.

From there they saw the grizzly paw
The meat-box door aside;
With wicked grin his head went in—
His body stayed outside.

Then Erling scratched a sulphur match,
It's light shone all around,
"Grrr!" said the bear, and did not scare
But dropped down to the ground.

"Oh, Erling, dash and get a flash!"
Cried Ottar in his glee!
"I will stay here—but do not fear
This Colt's enough for me."

Soon on the porch with flashing torch
Came Erling in full stride;
He quickly crossed, and then he tossed
The front door open, wide.

The flashlight shone—Ottar was gone!
Oh my, was that a jolt!
But perched above, just like a dove,
Was Ottar, with the Colt.

Meanwhile the bear who did not scare
Just took the meat away;
For, unafraid, he'd made his raid
And then did turn, at bay.

The flashlight's beam on him did gleam,
On eyes like balls of fire.
He ate the meat—it was a treat—
And then he did retire.

IV
URBAN BEARS
Garbage Dumps and Handouts

SHENANIGANS IN BANFF

$\mathcal{P}$at $\mathcal{B}$rewster

Pat Brewster was a member of one of Banff's pioneer families and grew up at a time when bears were becoming a big tourist attraction in the national park. One of his boyhood friends was Gordon Reed, son of Hayter Reed, manager of CPR hotels, and mother Kate, who was responsible for the interior design of the early hotel chain.

GORDON Reed some considered to be a spoiled boy, but I never agreed with their point of view for he always shared the many pleasures he received as a result of being the only child of a famous father and mother. For instance, his mother chartered a very nice motorboat for Gordon's private use the summer during which the following incident occurred. His cousin, Stewart Armour, and I used it whenever we felt inclined. We made many trips up the Bow River west of Banff and eventually, with some of my camping equipment, we established an overnight bivouac at a point opposite a rock shoulder that runs down from Sulphur Mountain to the Bow River.

The old town bridge used to cross the Bow River at a low level just east of where the present bridge is located. Immediately above the bridge landing on the south side, and well up on the hill, was the Brett Sanitarium Hotel where the Park Administration Building stands. A few hundred yards west on the road which leads to the Cave and Basin was "The Sign of the Goat Trading Company," run by Norman Luxton. Today it is known as the Indian Trading Post and it has changed little in appearance in all these years.

During the summer of 1908 Norman procured a bear from a trapper in Golden and brought it to Banff to keep in front of his store as a drawing card. The bear was fastened to a post by a fifteen-foot chain and walked continually about in a circle. People would gather on the perimeter of this circle and hand out bits of candy or biscuit to the bear. In this manner the bruin enjoyed a pleasant few hours each afternoon. It was a great novelty and attracted people from town as well as the guests from Bretton Hall and the Banff Springs Hotel. The bear was friendly and expected everyone to give him some little tidbit as he passed.

On our night in camp, Gordon busied himself with something he told us he had in mind, a little plan, but he could not tell us what it was. The next morning we made an exploratory expedition a bit farther up the river, and after lunch packed camp and pushed off for Mather's Landing on the Bow River at Banff. The boat was secured to the wharf and we proceeded up the road to Luxton's store.

In those days the Canadian Pacific Railway regularly sent picnic trains in the morning from Calgary to Banff which returned in the evening. One of those trains must have been in town that day because there were many people around the bear. Passing the captive animal, Stewart Armour and I gave our offerings which consisted of a small piece of bacon from the camp. Gordon Reed gave his tidbit as well. As soon as the bear had taken Gordon's offering, we proceeded on our way. There was not much commotion until we got onto the other side of the circle. The bear began to growl viciously. Suddenly he sprang into an upright position to stand on his hind legs, and gave one excruciating yelp, then started to run around in a circle growling all the time. The melee which followed is rather hard to describe. People started off in many directions and at various speeds. Several casualties resulted from this episode. One lady scrambling up the grass slope to the Brett Hotel tore the buttons from her dress; another man claimed that he tore his new suit in falling. The most remarkable complaint was reported by Dr. Brett who said that one friend sprained both his ankles as he tried to jump over a bank to avoid a stampede of visitors.

What was the cause of the incident? Gordon had loaded a chocolate with red pepper the night before up at the camp. This he had presented to the bear as his offering. The results were drastic. The Mounted Police were soon on the job and prevented Luxton from advertising in this manner in future. The bear did not eat much for the next few days, and would only accept food from his keeper. Luxton took the bear back to Golden and made a deal with a hotel keeper there to look after it. I believe that it lived for many years thereafter.

BEAR BITTEN

R.H. Stronach

The following testy letter was written by R.H. Stronach, Superintendent of Rocky Mountains Park, Banff, to Jasper Park Superintendent, Colonel Maynard Rogers, on 25 October 1923.

Dear Colonel:

THIS will acknowledge receipt of your telegram of 23rd instant, also the three bear cubs mentioned in this telegram. These cubs arrived this morning all in good condition and have been placed in our Zoo here. Many thanks for securing them for us.

In your letter to me of the 12th instant, you state these cubs are healthy and lusty, also that they are quite gentle although slightly mischievous, and I concur in all your remarks except the gentleness, as I was trusting enough to believe your statements regarding them, with the result that one bit my hand, but apparently it did not like the taste of a Scotchman and it only nipped out a small portion of my anatomy, but when it did so I do not mind telling you that I was extremely anxious that you should go to a place where you would have no further troubles through the price of coal or the shortage of heating facilities ...

With best wishes from all here, and again thanking you for sending us the bears.

BRUNO THE BEAR

from *Scarlet and Gold* magazine

This bear story was related by former Banff RCMP Sergeant H.C. "Casey" Oliver to an unnamed reporter of the RCMP's Scarlet and Gold *magazine in 1954.*

*B*RUNO was born at Lake Louise, Alberta, in the early spring of 1919. His mother, a very fine black bear having had a disagreement with a Dominion Government Game Warden, suddenly departed this life and became a very fine rug. Poor Bruno became an orphan.

The Game Warden presented Bruno, then being about two weeks old, to Sergeant H.C. (Casey) Oliver of the Banff Detachment, RCMP. Bruno took immediately to the bottle, (milk bottle) nipple and all, which with some sugar thrown in for flavour, was very greatly enjoyed by him. In his high spirits and appreciation of his sugar and milk Bruno raised havoc with the bottles so was provided with a tin pan for his milk and sugar ration. He thought it was a shower bath and so just threw it all over himself, his dining room being the basement of the detachment. One had to be careful in approaching when Bruno was dining as he stuck out in all directions with his now growing paws and claws much to the discomfort of nice highly polished jack boots, the owner of the boots being the discomforted one. Well, Bruno grew strong quickly and was provided with a good strong collar and a length of sash cord so he could be caught and handled when necessary.

He had quite a mind of his own. He liked certain chairs to sit in and objected when requested to move. However, he was the Sergeant's bear and that gave him some authority to do things not in accord with detachment regulations, or so he thought. Bruno was now growing, about two months old and was quite a free agent to wander around. He was well known in Banff and relaxed on the nice green lawn in front of the detachment. He did not interfere with anyone unless they interfered with him and he never left home except to wander over to the stable to fraternize with the horses and in a short time they got quite used to him.

One day Bruno was in his usual place, just in front of the detachment relaxing in the sun, when some four or five nondescript dogs, evidently habitants of Banff and incidentally running at large, held a conclave, decided that this strange animal, being a stranger, should not be allowed the privileges of a place like Banff and should therefore be attacked. They unanimously agreed on a mass attack and advanced in solid dog formation on Bruno, right on his own hearthstone.

Bruno quietly observed the attack developing, being quite a strategist himself. Did he run away? No sir, he simply hoisted himself on his hind legs and backed slowly up against the wall of the detachment where no rear attack could take place with fore arms swinging free and lightly at his side. There he awaited the charge of the aggressor dogs, which came alright, and as quick as a flash out went two good sized paws armed with growing claws and smote, smote is the word, the leaders of them thar dogs. The attack being over as far as they were concerned, they made a very hasty retreat in all directions, two of them howling to high heaven and if they had a spare paw it would have been used holding their jaws. Bruno, like a good soldier, or I should say policeman, just carried on, keeping an ever watchful eye on further possible assaults.

Bruno at times got in the way so one day things being busy he was taken by his little rope and although protesting, was shoved into one of the empty cells in the long cell room. The cell Bruno was in at the time had the usual little window with protection of iron bars, which are customary in such places, the window being opened for airing purposes. Bruno observed the little window, swung himself up to it and with some difficulty eased himself through the bars and lowered himself to the full extent of his arm. Holding onto the bars in the window and looking downward he decided the drop to the ground was too great a risk for a little fellow like him. He drew himself back again into the cell and being quite determined, he repeated the motion attracting the attention of many passers-by. Some Banff visitors thought they were seeing things.

At last one visitor came into the office to report that evidently a prisoner was endeavouring to escape. At that time there was quite a crowd of people watching the interesting spectacle and steps were taken to prevent Bruno's escape.

A short time after the above occurrence, Bruno was finding things rather dull the time being about 3:00 A.M., and seeing nothing interesting at home he decided on a walk. He strolled across the Bow River bridge and found opposite on the other side a most attractive building. It was the Bretton Hall Hotel, most inviting and restful. "Quite the place I have been looking for" thought Bruno, and ascending the hill towards the hotel he observed the ever open door of hospitality. The night being warm, the door was open and the night clerk was relaxing in his easy chair having a little snooze. The time was about 3:30 A.M. "Hi" says Bruno, "a nice place they run here" says he, and began ascending the grand staircase. All was quiet except for the nice homey snore of a weary and fatigued tourist enjoying the fresh mountain air. Contentment reigned supreme.

Bruno softly padded along the corridor and on coming to the end observed a door slightly ajar, the occupant wishing a little more fresh mountain air. Quietly he entered. The sleeper stirred, turned over, sat up and thought he saw something or someone sitting on the floor of his room. He suddenly sat up straight looked closer in the early morning dawn, the almost unbelieving sight of Bruno sitting there banished any further idea of sleep.

The guest now afraid to even move, was ready to pass out. To make a noise might even prove fatal. However, he gradually reached for the room telephone, phoned the office and the snoozing night clerk. "Come quick, help, a bear in my room quick, help!"

To help matters out, Bruno becoming a little frightened, bumped his way under the bed for safety and protection, thereby adding to the enjoyment of the occupant of the bed. "Oh go on", said the sleepy clerk, "What have you been drinking, I advise you to lay off the stuff." In due course the clerk did arrive at the guest's room and did observe movement under the bed and did recognize the Sergeant's cub bear. However, he thought it advisable to telephone the Sergeant. About this time all guests on the floor were awake and peeping through doors ajar.

At last the Sergeant arrived, caught poor old Bruno by his little rope and escorted him down the corridor and outside. The hub-bub in the hotel ever growing louder as guests scrambled to have a look, and search for any other wild animals that might be visiting guests in the hotel.

A very dear friend of Casey Oliver's, the Reverend Canon Montgomery, Rector of the Anglican Church of St. George's in the Pines, Banff, regales many tourists and especially American visitors with the story but embellishes it a lot giving action and colour to the incident, which is quite true and enthralls the listening tourist. The Canon ending his quite dramatic story with, "and there were all the guests of the Hotel, looking on from a distance and as the Sergeant said to the bear, 'what are you doing here, how dare you be here, and get out,' and the bear slunk off by itself down the stairs and out. All the guests acclaimed in a loud voice, 'how very wonderful, just think of it, even the wild beasts of the forest obey The Royal Canadian Mounted Police.'"

The bear, yes, what happened to the bear? A short time afterwards, Bruno now growing somewhat robust and becoming quite a charge, it was thought advisable that he be provided with a new home and under more restraint.

A Shrine patrol was passing through Banff to Portland where there was a Shrine Convention being held and behold they espied Bruno and saw a bright future for him as a Patrol Leader. So they negotiated for him and he was presented to the Patrol as a gift from the RCMP of Banff.

And so Bruno became attached to the Shrine Patrol and accompanied them on their long trek across the burning sandy desert to Seattle where it is reported he held up all traffic.

No news of Bruno for some considerable time, but if he lives up to expectations he will be a huge success. At any rate Sgt. Oliver has full confidence in Bruno's behaviour as a well trained member of the animal (wild) branch of the Force.

MOUTH-TO-MOUTH

C.E. Millar

WHEN wild animals and humans are close to one another continually, both lose some of their fear of the other. This is very true and also dangerous if the animals, especially bears, are given food. People who see black bears almost every day ... become used to seeing them around. They seem to lose a lot of their fear of these wild animals, as most of them are easily frightened away. This causes a few people to do unwise things. I think though, that the most hare-brained stunt with a bear that I ever heard about, happened in the late summer of 1929.

Cliff Fox was a bus driver, working for the Brewster Transport Company, driving a Grey Line bus from Banff to Lake Louise. He would generally stay there overnight, returning to Banff the following day. He was a good-natured man, full of wisecracks and flippant talk ...

Cliff knew that most of his passengers were photographers. Many of them had cameras hanging around their necks, ready for instant action. They wanted to take pictures of big game, and if he saw any that was close enough to be photographed, he'd stop the bus and let anyone off, if they wanted to take a picture.

A half-grown black bear used to wander along the highway between Baker Creek and Corral Creek, almost every day. He had been fed quite often, so he was a real pan-handler. He'd beg for food from anybody that came along. Cliff used to watch for him, and if he was lucky and saw him, he'd stop. He'd explain what he was going to do, and then he'd open the bus door and get out. Many of his passengers used to follow him.

When the bear approached him, he'd put a sugar cube on a spoon and let the bear eat it. This delighted the passengers and many of them took pictures of him feeding the bear. They were usually quite generous with their tips whenever this happened.

One day at noon, when we were both in the Brewster Transport Co's dining hall, I was talking to Cliff. I noticed that he had a small unusual looking scar near the tip of his tongue, so I asked him what had happened to make it. He explained that he'd had a slight mix-up with a young black bear, while people were taking pictures of himself and this bear. He said that the bear was standing on its hind legs, very close to him. It had taken a downwards swipe with one of its fore paws at him, and he'd stepped back in a hurry. In the excitement, he'd somehow opened his mouth, and his tongue must have stuck out, for the bear had put a claw right through his tongue, and that was the mark it had made.

He then stuck his tongue out and curled the end upwards to show me. I could see there was a small scar on the underneath side of his tongue, similar to the one on the top of it. What I couldn't understand was why the claw had made such a small, neat hole. It seemed to me that a claw would have made a ragged tear, if the paw had been descending, as he'd told me. The hole looked as if somebody had driven a nail straight down through Cliff's tongue. I made some remark about it being too bad, but I didn't make any comment about what I thought. I felt sure that there was more to the true story than what Cliff had told me.

I knew some of the Brewster drivers and a few days later I happened to hear a couple of them talking about Cliff's experience. I asked them what had really happened and they told me.

Cliff had been getting good tips from the shutter-bugs when they took pictures of him feeding the bear, so he thought he'd improve the act. He started sticking out his tongue and putting a cube of sugar on the tip of it, and letting the bear take it from there. This performance of danger and daring brought him even bigger tips at the end of the trip, so he made this stunt a regular one.

For a very short time everything went fine. One day, however, the bear bit Cliff's tongue, clamping down tightly with his long canine teeth.

Fortunately for Cliff, the bear opened his mouth again very quickly. He released the former's tongue, and then just took the sugar from it. That ended Cliff's days of feeding sugar on his tongue to a bear.

EDWARD'S GRIZZLY BEAR

Ken Jones

as told to Lorne and Kim Tetarenko

During the Depression years of the 1930s, Ken Jones often visited the Swiss Guides at the Chateau Lake Louise during the off-season. The guides led tourists to the summits of the peaks near the lake in summer, but after the CPR hotel closed for the season, they served as caretakers. The most colourful of these guides was the gnome-like Edward Feuz Jr., who first came to the Rockies from his home in Switzerland's Bernese Oberland district in 1903. Edward took his job seriously and could get very excited when things didn't go as planned.

*T*HE Chateau Lake Louise used to have a garbage pit at the back, with a road round it so the buses could drive around and let the people see the bears at the garbage. That was normal for those times. Every resort hotel had its garbage pit and its bears. The bears became very dependent on that garbage. The trouble was, every fall the hotel shut down and, you guessed it, no more garbage. But the bears were still hungry, and it was too early for them to go into hibernation, so they would come around and bamboozle everybody. They would try to break into anyplace where they could smell food. We managed to keep them from breaking into the Chateau, but they would often break into Deer Lodge and our guides' house. When we would finally manage to discourage them from bothering us, the bears would go down the hill to the town site and torment the people there. I recall one time when Ed Feuz—he was the impatient one—just got totally fed up with one particular bear.

It was early in September and I was at loose ends, so I travelled up to the Chateau with the Swiss guides. As happened every year, the bears would try to break into our guides' house first. That was because we arrived with fresh food, including meat, which probably smelled the strongest to them. We would spend every night for about three weeks to a month chasing those cussed bears away. Our problem was that we didn't have a cooler, so we had to keep some supplies outside. We should have used a storage shed with real strong walls, but I guess they did not have a bear problem in Europe, because the guides used a different method. They put the fresh meat and a few other supplies in a box and hung it from the roof of our building, on the front porch. The roof was quite high there, and we had a pulley system rigged up to raise and lower the box.

This particular year the bears seemed to be bigger and more aggressive than usual. In fact, they were really starting to get on everyone's nerves. Ed's in particular. During the night of this story's event we had spent several hours trying to chase four big grizzlies away from our front porch. They would growl and fuss, then seem to go away, only to be back a few minutes later trying to get at our cooler. Don't ask me why we had to keep that cooler on our front porch. I tried to tell them, but the guides were a stubborn lot; once they had an idea in their mind, it stayed there. Well, at last, about midnight as I recall, it seemed the bears had finally gone away, so we went to bed.

I shared an upstairs room with Chris Hasler, Walter Feuz was in the other upstairs bedroom, and Ed and Rudolph Feuz slept downstairs. I could always go to sleep right away, and once asleep I would never hear a thing. Actually, I did not know it at the time, but I was about fifty per cent deaf, so I guess that helped. About two hours later I woke up. Well, I didn't exactly wake up. I woke up because Chris was shaking me real hard. "Ken, Ken," he kept saying, "I think Ed's in trouble, wake up, wake up." Well, I finally woke up and we put on our slippers and went downstairs to see what was going on.

It was quite a sight. There was Edward spreading his climbing ropes all over the front room. He had about a mile of climbing rope in a big box in his room, so that was a lot of rope. Chris and I were used to Ed doing some funny things, but we were stumped on this one. As I recall the conversation went like this:

"Edward," exclaimed Chris, "what the hell are you doing now? What are the ropes for?"

Ed kept unravelling the ropes and replied, "I need them to pull the bear away."

"Bear?" Chris and I looked at one another, somehow we knew this was not going to be what we wanted to hear. "What bear, Ed?"

"Well, the son of a gun came back and was banging that meat box and the noise woke me up. So I got the .22 and shot at him. I thought it would scare him away, but I guess I hit him just right, 'cause he dropped right there."

Chris and I got Ed calmed down enough to tell us the story. It seemed he woke up, got the .22—it was the little single shot we kept for emergencies, without the Parks' people knowing, of course—opened the front window, stuck the gun out toward the bear and fired. He thought the noise would scare the bear away. Even if he hit it, he thought it would just sting him a bit and he would go away. But the grizzly just dropped in his tracks. He never made a sound or moved a muscle, so Ed was sure it was dead.

Chris and I decided we had better check this out. We were hoping that Ed was wrong. We did not want a dead grizzly to explain to the wardens, even worse, we did not want a wounded grizzly to explain. We could just see the problems—first, firing a rifle in the park, next, actually shooting something. No, this did not look good. Chris lit the gas lamp as there was no point in trying to do anything by the candle Ed had lit. We took the lamp to the window and tried to see if there really was a bear. Well, there was, and Ed was right. He was not moving, but Chris and I were cagey. I picked up some lumps of coal and leaned out the door to toss them at the bear.

He never budged, so we finally decided he was dead all right. Now what the heck were we going to do with a dead bear on our doorstep, right beside the Chateau Lake Louise, in Banff National Park? ... To make matters worse, Ed, just a few days before, had had a run in with the CPR about something. They had phoned him up and told him to do something, and he had said it was not something that we did, and so on. He was so mad at that time that he told us that he was going to quit. Well, now he was even more excited. He was jumping up and down about as high as the kitchen table.

"We gotta get him out of here and hide the body," he yelled. "The wardens will catch us and if they don't hang us, the CPR will fire us for sure." Chris liked to tease Ed, and couldn't resist telling him, "There's no point in your worrying about getting fired, you were going to quit three days ago anyway." It took us a few more minutes to calm Ed down again. Once we did, we started to talk about how we were going to move the bear. None of us gave a second thought to leaving him there or telling the Parks' staff. We knew we had to hide the critter.

We were all pretty excited by this time and it did not look like our discussion was getting anywhere, so Chris said, "Ken, you're a handy guy, maybe you know what to do. You tell us and we'll do it." I thought about it and said, "Let's get out the ropes and try to haul him away into the bush ... " So we got out the ropes, went out, and I fixed a loop around his head and neck, then tied his front feet tightly to the loop. That way we could pull him up head first. He would slide easier that way because the fur slopes to the back, and would not cause extra drag when we pulled him.

It was getting on to about four o'clock in the morning by now. We had to hurry because the Parks' people liked to drop by in the morning to chew the fat and have coffee with us. They did not have much to do at that time of year and they knew we were in the same situation. So none of us thought about getting dressed, or putting our rubber boots on. There we were, wearing our pajamas and bedroom slippers, with six inches of snow on the ground and it was raining to boot!

We finally got the bear—and he was a big one, well over five hundred pounds—trussed up and ready to move. He came off the porch and down the steps really easy, but then the fun began. The only place we could take him was into the bush close to the guides' house ... We decided to use the trail to the outhouse to best hide the skid marks, then continue from there into the bush. I did not really think we would get away with it; the carcass was bound to draw animals and birds, and any real outdoorsman would probably spot the signs a mile away.

Our troubles were just beginning. The path via the outhouse into the bush was uphill and it was a big bear. All our efforts to pull the critter led to a lot of sweat, but no progress. The snow was just too slippery and we could hardly walk, let alone pull the damn thing. Ed was getting excited again and hollering at us. Walter calmed Ed down by telling him, "Don't shout so much Edward, they'll hear you in Banff."

I stopped the boys and said we had better rig up a pulley system. So we rigged up a pulley system using a big tree as an anchor and a combination of two ropes. It wasn't difficult, as I just pretended that we were doing a mountain rescue with one whale of a sized mountaineer. But it was really slow going. It was at least two hours before we got that grizzly about a hundred yards into the bush ... Then we went back to the house. We were tired and soaking wet—not cold, mind you—we were working so blinking hard that we were actually steaming. I finished the job by taking a broom and sweeping over our tracks as best I could.

The next morning we went out and inspected our handiwork. Everything looked pretty good. There was no way to tell that we had dragged a grizzly up our outhouse path. We had breakfast and did our chores as usual, hoping that no Parks' people showed up, so we could all calm down as if nothing unusual was going on.

Anyway, when I finished the chores everything was quiet, so I thought I would go up and take a look at the bear in the daylight. When I got there I could see that he had a really nice hide. I pulled the hair and it was still tight. I thought it over for about one whole minute and said to myself, "What the heck, in for an ounce, in for a pound!" So I decided to skin the bear and take the hide. Yes, I know, this was now poaching in a national park, but it seemed a shame to waste such a good hide. I had just started when Chris came up. He had seen me head into the bush and guessed that I was going to check on our bear. Chris thought saving the hide was a good idea, so he pitched in and helped me skin it.

We were working away when trouble arrived in the form of Ed. He and Walter had noticed that Chris and I had disappeared and they knew darned well where we had gone. Ed did not want anything to do with any bear hide, especially skinning an illegal grizzly. Well, he and Chris talked for a bit about what a nice hide it was, and to my surprise Ed said, "You know, I wouldn't mind having a good grizzly hide. How much do you want for it?"

Chris gave me a wink and said to Ed, "It's going to cost you plenty for this one, Ed ... "

"So long as you don't go too high, I wouldn't mind having that hide," said Ed, and he went away to keep an eye out for visitors.

"Well," said Chris, "I think we should tell him five hundred dollars." Actually, neither of us wanted any money at all, we just didn't want to waste the hide, but we decided to egg Edward on and see how high we could get him to go. When we figured he had suffered enough, then we would give it to him and refuse his money.

Chris and I finally got that bear skinned and I took the hide to the laundry room. There I salted it, rolled it up in a sack and let the brine work through it. I used the laundry room because no one ever came there. I guess the CPR would have had a fit if they had known that I had used their laundry room to cure the hide of a poached grizzly. The amazing thing is that Ed normally could not hit a big barn door at ten paces with a shotgun, and here he was with his little .22, dropping a grizzly with one shot. Chris and I worked on the hide all winter, salting it, scraping all the fat out, then curing it some more. By spring we had that hide in really good shape. Ed watched our progress all winter, and as the hide got closer to being ready he got more and more interested. By spring he really wanted that hide.

When the roads opened in the spring, Chris came up in his car with his son Walter. They smuggled the hide out of the park in the trunk of his car, and took it to Golden. There he presented it to Ed, with the compliments of Chris and I. I did not want any money for it, but Ed gave Chris a twenty dollar bill to give me for my trouble.

BEARS IN JASPER

Nora Findlay

NOT many years ago the population of Jasper townsite was approximately two-thirds people and one-third bears. We all shared the streets of Jasper quite amicably and there were very few confrontations between the two elements of our society. At that time it would be a rare occasion to walk from your home to the downtown area without seeing a bear. The bears respected people and we respected the bears. If you happened to meet face to face, it was an unwritten law that you ignored each other. The bears knew it, and we certainly knew it.

The bears' affinity for town was the easy access to food. They preferred the alleys and foraged in every garbage can. We all tried to buy garbage cans with tight fitting lids, but the bears always out-smarted us. It was part of the daily stint of housekeeping to clean the alley each day, and place garbage back into the garbage cans.

Usually, in the spring, a bear would choose a three block area to become its home for the summer. If it was a mother bear with cubs, she knew which trees in that area were safe for her cubs while she foraged and fended off dogs.

One year in a particular neighborhood, we had a mother with three cubs. It was most interesting to watch her discipline her family. The cubs played: they got spanked and boxed by mom, and they learned to be very obedient. They learned never to come down from the tree until their mother told them it was safe. It was great entertainment for all of our guests.

At the east end of town, there was a mother bear with five cubs, nicknamed, "Mrs. Dionne."

One female decided to hibernate under a sort of ramp beside the railroad tracks. When she emerged in the spring, she had two beautiful cubs. Because they were born in town, that mother and her cubs adopted the main street as their territory. They all but learned to pose for the tourists.

A great deal of fear is associated with bears and I wonder why. There were no accidents that I know of. My most frightening experience happened on the first warm day of spring in 1943. I went out to my unfenced back yard with a blanket, a book, my baby and his bottle. We got nicely settled, he sucking on his bottle, and I, engrossed in my book. I heard a little grunt. When I turned my head, a bear was about one foot from my baby's head and the bear was chewing on the bottle. I gingerly and calmly picked up the baby and slowly walked to the house. Then the adrenaline started to flow and I very nearly collapsed.

Years later, the government issued an edict to all home owners that they were to provide garbage cans that could not be tipped over. It was interesting to see the variety of inventions the citizens came up with, but most of them couldn't fool the bears.

It was, however, particularly difficult for the "sanitation crew" to figure out how to dump these protected cans into the truck. Now all garbage is placed in large metal "bear-proof" containers. Our town is cleaner, but some of us miss our old neighbours, the bears, and the entertainment they provided.

THE NUISANCE GROUNDS

Hugh M. Halliday

Prior to the closing of open garbage dumps in the mountain parks in 1980, the "nuisance grounds" were a big attraction for park visitors. They were a guaranteed place to see bears, though hardly in their natural state.

FOUR or five miles out of Banff there is a small area that is favoured by Black Bears. It is known as the "nuisance grounds," which title, of course, is the euphonious name for the town garbage dump. Here, Denny Lynch, superintendent of the area, has been in charge for some 25 years. He divides his time between the burning of the garbage brought periodically from the town and supervising affairs related to the bears.

The last time I visited the "nuisance grounds" I left the road and cut through the bush. Following an old habit I came to rest beside a pathway and, sitting down, lolled back against a tree. Sunbeams, flecking through the foliage, caused me to shut my eyes. When I opened them a she bear was standing in the pathway; her feet were barely six inches from mine. A pair of small cubs were immediately behind her. She was looking intently into my face. Perhaps, as I remained dead still, she was wondering what "it" was and whether "it" was harmless. No doubt she had in mind the safety of her family. She moved along a few paces, stopped, looked back, and, as the cubs ran after her, disappeared around the hill.

Soon, another bear, a long-haired fellow of tremendous size, brushed by me. He was followed by two smaller, sleeker ones. As I watched I saw 13 bears converge on the garbage dump. It was not long before, in the distance, I could hear Denny Lynch doing a lot of talking. He was having bear trouble. While he was chasing one out of his little shack, another was pushing its way in. Finally, he got the bears all out and the door shut. But Denny was left inside and the moment he opened the door to come out himself another bear pushed in.

These bears know Denny as a kindly individual with a love for bears, even though at times he expends a lot of loud, threatening talk in their direction. Denny had known most of the bears that come to the dump since their babyhood, and some are becoming old and crotchety. But they have not forgotten Denny as their long-time friend. Nor have they forgotten how to steal into his cabin and run off with his lunch when his back is turned.

As a race, Black Bears are panhandlers. At every opportunity they become garbage-dump bums; they are the hoboes of the animal world. As Denny sits outside his little house and half a dozen bears crowd around, paying him homage by their loyalty and trust, he could scarcely be given a more fitting title than "king of the hoboes."

Immediately behind him is an old pine tree which perhaps has been climbed oftener by bears than any other tree in the world. It is still alive, but not much more. Its spreading branches have been polished bare of their bark by bears taking siestas among them. Denny relates that he has seen 16 bears dozing in this tree at one time, comprising four families of four in each family—an observation for the records, he thinks. They sit up there and stretch and yawn and indulge in bits of side play.

Denny says there are as many characters among his bears as among people. There are pleasant, happy bears, timid ones, grumpy ones, friendly ones, and bears that look at you out of a "fishy eye"—the ones with questionable intentions.

"Here come a couple of performing bears!" exclaimed Denny. "Watch them put on a show!"

A pair of sleek, two-year-old fellows moved out into the clear, stood on their hind legs, and exchanged cuffs, while a third climbed on top of a pile of stones, sat down, and faced the contestants as a spectator.

In the meantime, two boys, absorbed in the bears' scuffling, forgot to keep their eyes on their lunch and a bear got it. When they complained to Denny they were told it was against the rules to feed the bears and they had no business having food with them.

As we watched, some spectators, who had asked Denny where bears could be seen, finding themselves surrounded by bears, hurried to their cars and drove away. Bears have such soft pads on their feet they can walk right up behind you, nudge you under the arm, and nose into your pockets or handbag. Any parent would naturally suspect it was only his little boy becoming restless or hungry.

"Look at those contented bears out there," mused Denny, after the visitors had gone, "14 of them. I know them all. A person is safer among them than sitting in the bus station. See that really big fellow with the shaggy hair; he's been getting pretty crusty this last year or two, but I knew him when he was a little fellow climbing this tree. There are people who come in here who have never seen him before and they walk right up to him. One of these days we might have to shoot him because we have people who insist on annoying him when he wants only to mind his own affairs.

"Also I have heard those hot sultry days in August called dog days, but out here they are bear days. It is in August that the bears start coming around in numbers to see what I have for them. In July they are so busy harvesting bearberries that they haven't much time for me; but if I meet one of my bears in the bush, he knows who I am."

Denny says a black bear likes to mind his own business and if he does cause trouble a human being is in some manner at the bottom of it.

"See that old she bear out there pawing over the garbage? She won't bother you here; but go down the bank toward the tree where she left her cubs and watch how quickly she will follow—and you might not be in a good state of health when she is through with you either."

Denny says he does not think there is another baby animal living that has as much fun as a cub bear. He says they are just like people; when babies, they play innocently, and when half-grown they box, and wrestle, and climb trees like any boy. Also, they do as their mother tells them. As a parent she's the old fashioned kind. She spanks her cubs unmercifully if they disobey, but she will give her life defending them. Denny thinks if human parents brought their children up as well we would soon be able to close our jails.

All day Denny enjoys a front seat in the "bear ring." Trucks from town come periodically with garbage and between the burning of it and the bears, it is disposed of.

Denny says that if an old bear has only one cub with her she is not likely to be more than three years old. Older bears have families of two, three, four and, sometimes, five. Denny is sure of this because he has seen the cubs grow up, get into mischief, sit beside him in front of his cabin and eventually become parents—and later, grumbling old grandparents.

"And do you know," says Denny, "I think I would as soon live with bears as with people. Bears are awfully, awfully human in some of their ways. When a mother bear lays her big paw on the tender hide of a baby, being human, I feel like interfering, but I know that the old bear, being almost human, too, will resent my nosing into her family affairs, probably with a few well-placed rights and lefts across my ribs."

BEARS, ALL THE TIME BEARS

Rudy Wiebe

Even in the 1970s there was still a thin line between bear jokes and bear stories in the mountain parks.

WHY is it, all summer all you hear in the mountain parks is bear stories? I mean "stories" as in "jokes," so-called. Like the old klunker a otherwise pretty guide told us on the Maligne Lake boat cruise: How do you stop a bear from charging? Answer: Take away his credit card. And she expected us to laugh. Some idiots did.

You see more deer than bear in parks, but nobody tells stories that are supposed to be funny about them. Nor mountain sheep. They're pathetic, mooching along the highways all summer and nibbling junk from some kid's hand while mama shrieks, "Be careful—O—they're so cute!" and papa squeezes off another fifty feet of 8 mm. and then in fall with their digestion wrecked and the tourists gone, either the long-distance truckers wheeling through smash them or they go belly-up because there's no barbecued potato chips growing in the grass. I mean, I take pictures too, sure, but any junk food I buy my kids eat; their stomachs can take it.

My son—I only have one, also four girls, all older—my son Havre and I took that Athabasca River Raft Ride and there we heard the silliest bear story of all. You'd figure that for a two-hour ride at $12.75 per adult and $6.50 under twelve—since when is a thirteen-year-old adult?—they'd have quality stories when there's nothing but the usual scenery sliding past, which is most of the time with Edith Cavell sharp and frozen enough but looking more or less always the same in the background. Our raftsman with muscles like Pete Rose handles the raft's big sweep easy as a toothpick through rapids and you figure in the calm he'll come up with a man's story, but he pulls one out about a guide, four nuns, and a grizzly! They meet this big grizzly on a mountain path and the guide tells the nuns just keep calm and take one step back. They do, and the grizzly takes one step forward. The guide tells them just keep calm and take two steps back. They do, and the grizzly takes two steps forward. The nuns don't think too much of their guide's advice about then so they try their own technique: they kneel down and start to pray. And sure enough, the grizzly kneels down and folds his paws just like he's praying too and the nuns get real happy, see, he's religious, he won't bother us. "Nah," the guide says all grey and shaking, "he's the worst kind. He's just saying grace."

Some clods practically fall in the river laughing at that one. I had to give little Havre a bat, he was laughing too. We ran through the long rapids then just opposite Belchers Cabins and for a while that kept me busy hanging on with Havre yelling like a Red Indian and all the women aboard—I had sent my wife and the girls to take some good pictures of flowers—shrieking, grabbing their men like they wanted to throttle them right there in their own life jackets, but then I got to thinking: would that story have such a kick had it been a bull moose? No. And just tourists, not nuns? No again. The joke is in the danger: like this raft ride, you want to be scared but you want to know for sure it isn't really deadly—they tell you three times when you buy the raft ticket they've never lost a passenger yet, not even bust a neck—just the *feeling* of danger maybe. That's it, that *and* the religion: danger and making fun of religion, there you've got the biggest laugh multipliers of all. Kneel down to pray and nowadays somebody will kill himself laughing.

The wife says there are worse ways of going. That night a bear—no grizzly, just ordinary black but big enough that's for sure—a bear comes out of the bush by our campsite. I like to get close to nature and they give us a site—they've got over seven hundred of them, all full all summer—on the outer edge, right up against Whistler Mountain. So of course where does this bear come first?

One of my girls screams and two others drop their wieners into the fire and my wife says, "Into the truck, quick!" and shoos all five kids in the back there where we all sleep, but the bear doesn't come to us: he goes next door, number 29–A, where they've got a nice blue tent beside a table piled up with utensils and they've gone to see the nature film at the amphitheatre. That's the modern way, nature only happens on films. Anyway, it's 10:45 and this bear starts a rumble on that table and campers come running, gawking, and some idiot is taking flash pictures at sixty feet and I'm yelling at this bear to stop busting good equipment, waving my yellow plastic waterpail but he doesn't even bother to give me a side-glance until he's knocked everything over and it's clear there's nothing to eat there and without looking up he comes toward us, number 29–B, in that slope-shouldered easy sideways four-wheel-drive motion they have, ha! The wife and I are around the corner of the truck and the campers are screaming at their kids to get back and I peek around the corner and holy maloney there sits our silver 7-Up cooler! On the table, stuffed full of our breakfast. This flashes through my head and the bear is still coming—the campsites really are nicely spaced—and all of a sudden there's Havre out of the truck heading for the cooler too! Thank god the bear beats him to it. Havre's yelling and waving his arms like he was shooing a chicken and I've got him by the seat of the pants and throw him behind me and the wife catches him before his head bounces off the truck bumper and then that bear looks me in the eye: his two front paws are up on the cooler but it's good stuff, it doesn't open or bend and when I throw the water from my pail at him his head swings up and he looks at me and I know he'll charge, never mind the credit cards, and I try to scramble back, scrunch, and of course I fall flat on my can.

You know that old one about your whole life flashing by before your eyes? Forget it. When you look into the little close-together eyes of a black bear swinging his head around mad, your ticker stops dead and there's nothing but simple flush-everything-out-in-one-woosh terror. I'm on my back, my wife is grabbing for my arm and screaming, Havre is screaming, the girls are all screaming in different keys and I'm trying to move and I don't know if I'm still alive and I *am* still alive because the bear has not charged!

The screams don't matter to him. He has knocked that 7-Up cooler off the table and is rolling it backward under the trees, end over end,

109

and walking backward like a circus dog doing tricks and finally the lid pops off and he stops, fifty feet away, to have a look. Four pounds of hamburger, two of bacon, a dozen eggs, two loaves of bread, butter, four quarts of milk, mayonnaise: could be worse. He settles down right there and has a picnic. Half an hour; nobody, but nobody bothers him.

Eleven-fifteen; out on the prairie it would still be light but against the mountain we can barely see him, nothing but a dark blotch when he pushed the cooler away, stands up and swings his head around, then continues on to 29–C, 29–D, perfectly alphabetical. But everybody's stowed everything in their vehicles and he's sniffing around 29–M when the ranger finally gets there and throws a firecracker at him that explodes like a cannon and he, without any rush but like that were some sort of signal, lopes off sideways into the dark. He'll be back now, the ranger says looking at me sour as pickles, tomorrow for sure and they'll have to try and shoot him with a tranquillizer and haul him way back into the mountains.

So I got dirty looks besides all the embarrassment. When our neighbours got back from their nice nature film about twenty people told them why their equipment was so messed up and then they all looked at me trying to bend my cooler straight—all that was left in it was the jar of mayonnaise, open but uneaten—and sort of chuckled. We pulled out for the Columbia Icefields real early next morning. And I'll tell you one thing. If I ever hear some guide tell a story about some hell-fire preacher in a big Winnebago trying to shoo away a bear rattling empty cans at his neighbour's while he's got a full hamper of food standing right beside him, I won't be held responsible for what happens.

V

TALL TALES OR TRUE?

Strange and Fabulous Stories

THE MAN-EATING BEARS
OF YARROW CREEK

Andy Russell

Growing up near Waterton Park in southwest Alberta, Andy Russell was exposed to a number of bear stories that had become part of the folklore of the region. The Stoney Indian legend of man-eating bears in the Yarrow Creek valley is a remarkable tale that Andy could never corroborate or disprove. But if the Stoneys were right, was the trapper Slim Lynch killed by the descendants of this murderous clan?

P ERHAPS the strangest story ever circulated in our mountains was told by an old Indian chief many years ago to my father-in-law, Bert Riggall, one of the pioneer outfitters and guides in the Alberta Rockies, a recognized naturalist and botanist. When Bert Riggall first came to this section of the country with a survey party in 1903, a big party of Stonie Indians were camped on Cottonwood Creek about a mile north of our present home. The Indians were an offshoot of the Assiniboin tribe of the Assiniboine Mountains in Manitoba. They were excellent mountain hunters, who made their climbing moccasins from the thick, spongy hides of mountain goats and ranged up among the peaks above the hunting grounds of the Blackfeet.

The Stonies were methodical, well-organized hunters, who perfected a most effective system of driving in pursuit of mountain game. While the squaws, youngsters, and old people went into the valleys with numerous dogs, the braves deployed along high trails crossing the ridges and passes. Sometimes they used natural cover for a hide, but if such was not suitably located, they built blinds of loose stones close to the game trails. At a signal a great din was set up by the drivers and their dogs that was sufficient to send the game animals scampering for the heights. There they ran into the ambushes and were sometimes slaughtered in piles along narrow defiles. Bert Riggall recorded that the party on the Cottonwood packed out forty pack-horse loads of dried jerky and buckskin when they left. This represents a considerable number of animals the size of deer and sheep; for there was practically no bigger game left in the country at the time. Consequently, when Bert took up his homestead on the Cottonwood shortly after, he found lean hunting. One valley, Yarrow Creek canyon, was an exception. No Indian trails penetrated its thickly wooded bottom, and it teemed with bighorns and mule deer.

Bert was friendly with the senior Stonie chief, King Bear's Paw, and when the old man heard he was hunting the Yarrow country, he made a long ride to warn Bert of a peril. Yarrow Creek valley was taboo to the Indians. The old chief told a tragic story of the origin of the taboo.

About 1860 most of the Stonie tribe was gathered in a great wintering camp on the edge of the mountains along the Bow River, just east of where Banff National Park is now located. Their lodges were pitched on ground later to become their reservation. During the winter they were stricken with smallpox, the dread disease introduced by white men. Having no resistance to it and understanding nothing of its treatment, the Indians died like flies. Very early in the spring a party of still healthy survivors packed their travois and fled south, trying to escape the scourge. They set up their teepees on the flat where Yarrow Creek debouches from the mountains. But they carried the infection with them, and this camp was soon paralyzed with sickness. The Indians became so demoralized and helpless that they could not even dispose of their dead in the usual fashion; they just dragged the bodies of unfortunate relatives and friends into the brush on the edge of camp and left them to rot.

The bears were just coming out of den, hungry as usual, and were inevitably attracted by the constant smell of carrion. As King Bear's Paw recounted, the grizzlies began by feeding on dead bodies, and then growing bolder, they came right into camp to take Indians not yet dead and even to attack some few survivors. These understandably panicked and stampeded, leaving the place to the bears. To this day no Stonie has ever made a moccasin track in Yarrow Creek canyon again.

"The bears are very bad there," King Bear's Paw warned. "They have tasted the meat of men. Stay out of that country."

Bert recognized and appreciated the old man's concern. He gave him some small presents of tea, tobacco, and sugar, thanked him solemnly, and assured him that he would be very careful and that his bear medicine was very strong. Shaking his head, the chief left.

One day not long afterward Bert was back in the canyon cutting trail through some heavy growth of wind-twisted pine and spruce. He was chopping a way through a tangle below a series of shelving rock ledges when he noticed his horse, ground-hitched a few yards behind him, suddenly throw up its head and stare fixedly at something on the slope above. Bert could see nothing from his position, so he went back and mounted his horse for a better view. To his astonishment he saw two big grizzlies sneaking stealthily down through the low scrub growing on the ledges toward the spot he had just left.

They did not see him till he yelled. Then they milled around with their hair up, alternately rearing and snuffling, while he sat his saddle with his rifle cocked and ready. It was an early vintage .30–30, and at that moment it seemed a very inadequate arm. Bert knew that shooting one grizzly in such a place would very likely bring both animals down on him, so he held his fire. Finally the grizzlies departed. Bert was never quite sure if they were drawn by curiosity or if they had some mischief in mind. From then on, while working alone in the canyon, his rifle was always within easy reach, and on occasion he found use for it.

Some fifty years after the grizzlies' raid on the Indian camp in Yarrow Creek another incident occurred, in the spring of 1912, that at first glance seemed to corroborate a grizzly propensity for eating human flesh.

A trapper by the name of Slim Lynch was working the lower valley of Kishaneena Creek, about thirty miles west of Yarrow valley. He was the foster son of a widower by the name of Beebe, who, with three grown sons and Slim, was trapping the tributaries of the North Fork of the Flathead River in the vicinity of the International Boundary.

Slim had a line cabin built near extensive beaver colonies about ten miles up Kishaneena Creek on the Canadian side of the border, and he was busy harvesting pelts when trouble arrived. The trapper had been skinning the beaver at his cabin and carelessly discarding the carcasses in the nearby timber. No smell will draw a grizzly like the odor of fat, half-ripe beaver. A big silvertip moved in on this bonanza of feed, and as time passed the bear grew bold. Slim carried only a belt gun and quite likely was worried about the bear breaking into his cabin during his frequent absences and ruining his stockpile of pelts. So he tied the furs on a packboard and snowshoed out to his main cabin on the Flathead. He told his foster father about the bear and said something about setting a gun for it.

At that time the set gun was a common and effective way for trappers to take a grizzly. Such a gun was light and compact and could be carried in a backpack much easier than an adequate steel trap. Although some set guns were specifically designed and manufactured for the job, most trappers manufactured their own simply by shortening the barrel and stock of a cheap single-shot twelve-gauge shotgun. The gun was fixed in the apex of a v-shaped pen built of logs, with a couple of small trees growing close together enclosed in the small end of the pen. A nail was put through a hole bored for that purpose in the butt of the gun and driven into the rear tree. The barrel was then lashed solidly to the tree in front so that it pointed towards the open end of the enclosure. A string was run from the trigger back over a convenient knot or another nail behind the gun and then forward over a crossbar fixed just in front of the muzzle, where a bait was hung on the end of it. The gun was cocked to make it ready for a tug on the bait, which would send a lethal lead slug or charge of heavy buckshot into the head of the victim that had been decoyed into position. Many a grizzly thus ignominiously shot himself.

Either Slim forgot to take a regular set gun, or he decided to use his Luger automatic pistol, a recently acquired weapon that was the last word in side arms at the time. He lashed his pistol at the back of a log pen built for the purpose, hung a juicy piece of beaver meat on the trigger string, and retired for the night to his cabin.

Sometime in the night the trapper was jerked awake by the sharp crack of the pistol. Slipping his feet into his moccasins, he went out into the moonlight to investigate. The clearing in front of the cabin was lit up like day, but there was no sign of the grizzly. Upon examining his set, Slim found that the tug on the string had somehow tipped the short gun in its lashing before it fired, so the bullet went harmlessly high.

Anticipating the return of the grizzly, he was in a hurry to reset the gun and made a fatal mistake. Somehow he forgot the pistol was an autoloader, and while he was adjusting another bait, his hand slipped and instantly orange flame stabbed at him from the muzzle of the gun. The 9 mm. cupronickel-jacketed bullet plowed into his stomach and out his back under a shoulder blade. Mortally wounded, the trapper managed to stagger back to his cabin, where he collapsed on his bunk.

What happened then was for many years fogged by the exaggeration and dramatization of a story told and retold around countless campfires. Presumably the grizzly came back and, striking the fresh blood trail leading into the cabin, followed it. Pressing through the open door, the bear grabbed the trapper off the bunk. The desperate man clutched at bedding and bunk, which was smashed, torn, and strewn across the cabin floor. The bear dragged his victim outside and killed and ate him. Later a search party found his scattered remains and buried them at the foot of a big western larch near the cabin.

When I first heard this story, I believed it; but later a better knowledge of grizzly character made me wonder. In the summer of 1952, forty years after the tragedy, I was guiding a party of geologists on the upper reaches of the Flathead in British Columbia, where I met and came to know a very remarkable man by the name of Charlie Wise. Charlie was then seventy years old, but he carried his six-foot frame as straight as an arrow and still followed his wilderness trapline. A very trustworthy and keen-minded man, he told me the facts of the Slim Lynch story.

About the time of Slim's unfortunate accident a warm, heavy downpour began that lasted several days. Augmented by fast-melting snow, the Kishaneena and other creeks feeding the Flathead River were soon roaring over their banks and the river itself was a berserk flood of completely impassable waters. When Slim failed to show up as expected, the Beebes naturally supposed he had been cut off by the floods and were not unduly concerned at first. But when the waters began to go down and still Slim failed to make an appearance, they set out to look for him, accompanied by Charlie Wise.

The mounted search party had considerable difficulty fording their horses across still-swollen streams, but finally they managed to reach Slim's cabin. Immediately they knew something was desperately wrong. No smoke came from the chimney, the door hung awry, and there was a sickly smell of death in the air. The interior of the cabin was a shambles. Mixed with a mess of debris in front of the cabin they found the pitiful remains of Slim—thigh bones, skull, pelvis, and a few other fragments. The pistol was still set in its pen, loaded and cocked, ready to blast anything that pulled the string. A dark-stained wool undershirt with a bullet hole front and back was found. Bit by bit they found evidence telling the grim story.

There were two cartridges missing from the pistol magazine, and on the ground were two empty cartridge cases, which indicated that the gun had been fired twice. Because Slim had reported a grizzly on his visit to the base cabin, they knew a grizzly bear was involved, although all sign was washed away by the flood. They did find some fresh black-bear tracks. The original story was correct except that Charlie Wise was convinced that Slim had been long dead, when a black bear, not a grizzly, had raided his cabin, torn the trapper's body to pieces and eaten it.

Because the trail to the nearest settlement was impassable and no official could be immediately contacted, they buried what was left of Slim under a huge tamarac and marked the grave with a blaze. The blaze is still visible on the old tree beside the ruins of the cabin. Later Slim's remains were exhumed and reinterred in the cemetery at Columbia Falls, Montana.

SPEAKING OF BEARS

Lawrence Burpee

Sitting around the campfire at night on the trail, the conversation inevitably turns to bears. And as Lawrence Burpee discovered on a trip up Jasper's Whirlpool Valley in the 1920s, it is often hard to separate fact from fiction.

Speaking of bears," I said, "do you see many grizzlies in the park?"

"We weren't speaking of them," replied the Warden.

"However, we do run across them occasionally, and occasionally they run across us. One of our fellows had a queer experience last spring. He was working in the corner of his cabin with his back to the door. Heard the door open and slam to. He called 'Hello!' thinking it was one of the men. Getting no answer, he glanced over his shoulder—and made a quick grab for his gun. A grizzly had pushed in through the door, which shut to after him. The bear could see no way out, felt he was trapped, and turned savagely toward the man. The man was in a devil of a scrape. The bear was between him and the door, and he knew that if he tried to wriggle through the window the bear would certainly get him. Fortunately he was a good shot, and kept his head. The skin made a fine floor-mat."

"That reminds me," I said, "of a story Ross Cox tells in his *Adventures on the Columbia*. It appears that in the spring of 1816 a party of fur-traders had been sent down the Flathead River. One evening while they were quietly sitting around a blazing fire eating a hearty dinner of deer, a large, half-famished bear cautiously approached the group from behind a large tree, and, before they were aware of his presence, he sprang across the fire, seized one of the men round the waist with his two forepaws, and ran about fifty yards with him on his hind legs before he stopped.

"The man's comrades were so thunderstruck that for some time they lost all presence of mind, and ran to and fro in a state of fear and confusion, each expecting in his turn to be kidnapped. At length a half-breed hunter, Baptiste Le Blanc, seized his gun, and was in the act of firing at the bear, but was stopped by some of the others, who told him he would certainly kill their friend in the position in which he was then placed.

"Meanwhile the bear had relaxed his grip of the captive, whom he kept securely under him, and very leisurely began picking a bone which the latter had dropped. Once or twice Louisson attempted to escape, which only caused the grizzly to watch him more closely; but, on his making another attempt, he again seized Louisson round the waist, and commenced giving him one of those infernal embraces which generally end in death.

"The poor fellow was now in great agony, and gave voice to the most frightful screams. Seeing Baptiste with his gun ready, he cried out, '*Tire! tire! mon chere frère, si tu m'aimes. Tire, pour l'amour du bon Dieu! À la tête! À la tête!*' This was enough for Le Blanc, who instantly let fly, and hit the bear over the right temple. He fell, and at the same moment dropped Louisson, but gave him an ugly scratch with his claws across the face, which for some time afterward spoiled his beauty. After the shot Le Blanc darted to his comrade's assistance, and with his hunting-knife quickly finished the bear, and pulled Louisson out from under him, pretty thoroughly frightened, but otherwise not much the worse for his experience, barring the scratch."

"Humph!" grunted the Warden. "Where d'you say you got that yarn?"

"Ross Cox," I replied, "the old fur-trader after whom that peak above the flats was named. He came through here in 1817, going east, and wrote a pretty good book on the fur trade. More human than some of them. Don't you believe the bear story?"

"Oh, may be," said the Warden cautiously. "A bear might do that sort of thing if he was starving. Usually they keep away from a fire. Of course rum things sometimes happen. There was a trapper had a narrow escape last year. He had had a heavy day, found himself a long way from camp at sundown, and slept behind a log. He was tired, and slept later than usual. Finally a noise woke him, and he found himself looking up into the gaping jaws of a huge grizzly, which was straddled over him.

"He knew that if he made any sudden movement he was done for. His gun was beside him, but the chances of using it were mighty slim. However, he must make the attempt. It was that or nothing. Very slowly and cautiously he drew it into position, freezing into rigidity whenever the bear grew suspicious. Finally he let fly, and pretty near blew the old fellow's head off. By great good luck he kept clear of the claws, but pretty nearly had the life crushed out of him when the heavy body came down on top. Managed to pull himself clear finally, more dead than alive, and an awful sight."

The Warden refilled his pipe, lighted it with a burning twig, and remarked, "Bears certainly are queer cattle. There was Pete, now, over on the Miette. He walked into his cabin one morning an' found a bear lying on his bed. Pete slammed the door after him and ran round to the front, only to meet the bear coming through the window. He yelled and the bear growled, and they both beat it in different directions."

I glanced at the Warden reproachfully. "Whose leg do you think you're pulling?" I asked.

The Warden got up, stretched himself, knocked the dottle out of his pipe and put it in his pocket. "A man," said he disgustedly, "can tell lies by the yard, and get away with it; but when he's telling nothin' but God's unvarnished truth some tenderfoot is sure to doubt his word." And he vanished into the tent.

IT'S GOOD TO BE ALIVE

N. Vernon-Wood

Nello "Tex" Vernon-Wood was a British expatriate who emigrated to Canada and was hired as one of Rocky Mountains (Banff) Park's early wardens in 1915. Later he worked as an outfitter and hunting guide and wrote numerous articles for sporting magazines in his trademark cowboy vernacular style. This piece, which appeared in National Sportsman *in September 1936, relates how the hunter can sometimes become the hunted ... or at least the haunted.*

*J*T looks like another one of them swell days when Ol' Sol pokes his snoot over the mounting an' says Good Morning all over our camp. It's Indian Summer, an' there's a smell in the air that sort of makes yore hair bristle, an' you want to go out an' slap a Grizzly's face just to see if he's got nerve enough to do something about it.

At least, it seems to affect my Pilgrim that way. He's sittin' cross-laigged by the fire, scalin' flapjacks down as fast as Greasy can slide 'em off'n the skillet, an' breathin' deep of the mornin' ozone like he was takin' exercises.

"Tex," says this Pilgrim around the edge of a flapjack, "you know it's worth five hundred Gold Standard dollars, just to be alive this morning."

Which is *his* way of lookin' at it. There's a blister on my heel, left over from scalin' a few thousand perpendiculous feet of slides the day previous; I got a hangnail that don't feel so good, an' besides, I'm not addicted to deep breathin' of a mornin', so I just grunts. Bein' alive don't seem any better today than it did yesterday, an' yesterday I found the beginnin' of a crack in the stock of my favorite rifle.

"Mebbe," I growls, thinkin' of the blister an' the crack, "but I druther see the five hundred."

• • •

Me an' the Pilgrim got going right celerious after breakfast, an' high-tailed for the slides, an' the general direction of a Wapiti we'd heard trumpetin' earlier in the mornin'. By ten o'clock the O' Hay-maker has melted the frost, an' it's warm enough to peel off our sweaters. There ain't a mosquito or hoss fly in six townships, an' on the slides the huckleberries are thick as sextenarians at a Townsend picnic. We're depletin' the visible supply when that Elk let out a holler so close I thought he was in my pocket. The Pilgrim grabbed his rifle, an' we both looked in fourteen different directions, when I caught the glint of sun on the ivory-white tips of his antlers, an' silently pointed.

As we watched, the Elk stalked out into the open, an' I begun to laff. It's a young Bull of eight points, narrow in the spread, an' right spindley in the beam, but man, oh man, has he a voice? To hear him, you'd think he rated a fifty-inch spread an' fourteen points. Which, when you come to think of it, is another point of similarity between us sapiens an' the rest of the mammalia.

So leavin' almighty-voice to accumulate years an' spikes, we oozed along, up an' on, over scree slopes, around scrub balsam patches, an' through larch groves. We're settin' on an outcrop, catchin' up our wind, an' watchin' for somethin' to show up; way below us, Leman Lake looked like a big turquoise layin' on green velvet, an' here an' there, the golden brown of the slide grass run up to the silver gray of the limestone. The Pilgrim is takin' on somethin' epic about Nature's Canvas, an' the color harmony of Sky, Lake, an' Forest, when I seen somethin' that made me jab my elbow into his ribs, shuttin' off the flow of rhetoric.

Standin' out on a two-bit bench about three hundred yards away, an' slightly downhill, is a perfectly good Elk. He's as still as a bronze image an' watchin' somethin'. Then I see, way down in the crick bottom, a half-dozen cows pokin' along footloose an' fancy free.

The question immediately arises will we take a poke at him right now, or shall we try to stalk closer, meantime runnin' the chance of his decidin' to constitute himself a welcomin' committee of one, an' go tearin' down to thrill them females.

A bird I'm guidin' one time promulgates the theory that a successful hunter has to try to think like he thinks the beast he's huntin' thinks. If you get what I mean.

So, I think—here I am, a right personable batchelor Wapiti, with plenty of free time and no place special to go, and yonder's a bunch of beautious gals, down there by the crick. An' I see myself tearin' down the slide, knockin' over some right sizeable timber in my onseemly haste—so I says to the Pilgrim, "About three hundred an' don't forget it's a downhill shot, so aim low."

• • •

It's a shame to nip romance before it's budded, but we need that trophy, an' the .30–06 Springfield, with a certain amount of co-operation from my Dude, done it.

"An' now," I says, "you can turn loose your flow of declamation relatin' to nature's palette all you like, while I perform several major operations on that beast."

There's a heap of awful good chewin' on a Elk, an' when it comes to salvagin' meat, I'm a reg'lar Indian. Nothin' burns me up like the eggs who drop a prime animal, an' then just saw offen the head, an' leave the meat for the Coyotes an' Wolverines. By the time I've dessected the kill, an' hung up the steaks an' roasts to cool, the shadows are gettin' long.

I got the head on my shoulders, an' we hit for the valley. There ain't any trail, so I'm watchin' my footin', an' not payin' any attention to what's goin' on elsewhere. The Pilgrim, bein' burdened only with the liver an' a couple of back strips, is checkin' over the slides, an' suddenly says, "Tex, I'd swear there's a Bear on that second opening to the left."

I dropped the Elk head, glad of the chance, an' fished my binoculars out of my shirt front. "Yeah—it's a Bear all right all right," I said after a look. "Either a fair Black or a small Grizzly—wait until he turns—yeah, it's a Grizzly, but he ain't such a much."

"He looked big to me," says the Pilgrim. "Are you sure you're lookin' in the right place?"

"Well, I'm lookin' at a Bear, but from where I stand, he don't look like any rug for your liberry. He might make a couple pair of fur-lined garters for a small chorus gal," I reply. "What you want to do—go get him or leave him lay?"

"Let's stalk it, anyway."

So I hung the Elk head in a spruce, an' we started to climb, anglin' toward the second slide. When we got to the edge of the timber we snuck up, an' checked over the open slopes. Nothin' in sight, up, down or across. What to do? Go higher, or slip down keepin' in cover of the trees? I'm all for the latter for various reasons, the main one bein' that it's in the general direction of camp, an' them matutinal flapjacks an' bacon have long ago been burnt up producin' energy for luggin' twelve-point Elk heads over the surroundin' terrain. But I bluff the Dude that it's logical for a Bear to travel downhill for evenin' vespers.

• • •

At that I'm right. We hadn't gone five hundred yards when we seen a clump of willow bush wavin' to an' fro, with no wind to agitate it. Somepin' in it, shure as hell is a man trap. Before I could spit, the bear showed part of him clear, and the Pilgrim cut loose. At the second shot Bruin come out of the bush, half rollin' an' half runnin'. Whammy—the Springfield sings out agen, an' the Bear flopped an' stayed put. We eased up, careful to see was he out, or just playin' possum until we was in rushin' distance.

It's a small Grizzly, an' not much of a trophy, as trophies go, altho' I've seen smaller ones that left this part of God's country addressed to the Taxidermist.

The Dude is feelin' kinda six-for-a-nickel. He looks at the Bear kinda thoughtful, an' says, "How wouldja like a new rug for the livin' room floor?"

I see what he's drivin' at, so I says as nonchalant as hell, "My missus asked me to accumulate some kinda hide to cover the hole in the livin' room rug, an' this'll just about fit. Tell you what. While I go to work on this schoolboy, you amble back to camp with the liver an' tell ol' Greasy that I'll be 'bout half an hour behind you, an' that about a pound of liver cut thick, rolled in corn-meal, an' fried not too much in deep fat, with a side order of fool-hen, a quart of java, an' plenty boiled rice an' raisins is what my system craves."

I guess the Pilgrim was lookin' for an excuse to fade from the scene of his infanticide, because he didn't even argue.

It's dusk by the time I am ready to hit for camp. I'd left the head in the hide, figurin' to skin that out in camp. I shoved the works into my ruck-sack an' began movin'. When I got to the foot of the slide, it was dark.

• • •

Did you ever have that spooky feelin' that somebody or something is doggin' you? Most generally, I've got the nervous temperament of a mud turtle, but somehow that evenin' I don't feel as placid as usual. Then I heard a faint snap behind me, like somethin' broke a small twig. I turned, quick, an' man oh man, I felt my heart jar my bridgework.

Not twenty feet behind me was a real Grizzly. It was nine feet high an' twenty-four feet long, an' three ax handles an' a plug of eatin' tobacco between the eyes. Anyhow, that's how it looked first time. When I turned, it stopped an' just set.

"An' now what?" I thought. I ain't got any rifle, an' somehow I can't see myself engagin' hand to hand with a Grizzly b'ar.

Men an' bretherin, I'm here to tell you that the hardest thing I ever did in forty-odd misspent years, was to turn my back on that Horribilis, an' go on down the trail, tryin' to kid myself that calmness an' coolness was the ticket. I'm tryin' to make that Bear believe that havin' him tag me along was nothin' onusual, an' that blame thing done just that. Ever' so often I'd take a quick look behind, an' there it'd be, two jumps behind, an' still comin'. I expected to feel his teeth in my off ear any minute. I wonder if it's the mother of the precocious adolescent I've got on my back, an' if so, just when she'd decide to work me over, or is it just another Bear that's mebbe attracted by the phenominum of perfectly good Bear smell all mixed up with man-scent. It's a academic question that I druther was more hypothetical right now. All I know is, the only Bears I'm goin' to like from now on are those that are laid out, harmless an' tee-totally defunct, an' ready for the skinnin' knife.

I wanted like hell to run, but what's the use? The Bear can overtake me in three jumps, an' anyhow it's no sign of a gentleman to be in a hurry. I want to shout, but my mouth an' throat is dry as the Mojave

Desert. I'm shiverin' an' sweatin' an' cussin' an' wishin' I knew more prayers.

When we finally got to where the crick we'd been followin' run into the river, it's a leetle lighter. The valley is more open, an' the stars are out, an' I think how peaceful an' safe-like the crick looked when we forded it a few days back.

I take another quick look behind, an' see the Bear, still on my trail. I wish my daddy had trained me for the Ministry, but what's the use? Then across the river I seen the flicker of our campfire, an' heard the faint tinkle of the horse bells. I dunno why, but that seemed quite a help. I don't waste any time lookin' for a ford, but hit the river just where I was, figurin' I'd just as leaf drown as be dessected. I was shirt pockets deep a couple of times, an' this'n is a glacial river, but that evenin' I didn't know if it was freezin' or boilin'.

About two hundred yards from camp, I managed to let out a sort of croak, an' the Pilgrim an' ol' Greasy hollered back. I sat down then to stop my knees from shakin' plumb out of their sockets, an' to let my hackles smooth down, an' generally catch up on my sang froid.

• • •

That night we was loafin' around the campfire. I'd had a couple quarts of coffee, as well as the liver an' fixin's. Life is lookin' some better than it did that mornin'. The blister ain't as bad as a broken laig, an' I figger a crack in a rifle stock ain't goin' to lose me no Trophies in future hunts.

Says the Pilgrim again: "Tex, I still say it's worth about five hundred Gold Standard dollars, just to be alive an' out in the hills."

I shuts my eyes hard a minute, an' right away I see that she-Grizzly on the trail behind me. When I open 'em again I says, real fervent-like, "Pilgrim, you tellin' *me*?"

THE JUMPING BEAR

Walter Nixon

as told to Bruno Engler

Not long after mountain guide-photographer Bruno Engler emigrated to Canada from Switzerland, he spent some time with outfitter Walter Nixon at his trapper's cabin in the Simpson Valley. One evening Walter decided to thrill this newcomer to the Rockies with a bear story.

ONE clear, moonlit evening—it must have been 20 to 30 below, I was in my bunk fast asleep. It was after midnight. Something woke me up. I thought it was somebody knocking at my door.

It was darn cold and I was not inclined to get out of my warm bunk. I yelled at whoever was out there to lift the latch and come on in. I got no answer so I shouted out my greeting a few more times. Still no answer …

Finally, I got up. My legs were stiff with rheumatism. I walked over to open the door. When I swung the door open, I saw a huge grizzly ready to jump on me. I ducked and that bear went right over me. I ran outside, shutting the door behind me. I was only in my long underwear and it was bitterly cold. Now the grizzly was inside and I was outside. Boy, was it cold! The blue light of the moon was shining on the snow. I could hear the bear inside my cabin, knocking stovepipes and dishes all over the place. Finally, I couldn't stand it anymore. I was freezing. I had no choice. My rifle was just inside the door. I had to make a dash for it or freeze to death …

In desperation, I made my move. I opened the door and reached blindly for my gun. The bear was coming at me, ready to pounce. I ducked again, and the bear went over me just like before except this time he landed outside. I quickly shut the door on him. Now the bear was outside and I was inside. I bolted the door and wrapped a blanket around me. I never thought I'd be warm again. I looked out the window and guess what I saw? ... In the light of the moon on the brightly lit snow, this big grizzly was out there practising his short jumps.

A BEAR OF A STORY

from the Banff *Crag and Canyon*, 7 May 1975

OVERHEAD in the library during tea time some time ago was a bear story with a bite ...

It seems Jim Thorsell was walking along a hill in the eastern end of the park when he heard some noises coming from below the hill. He ran to the edge of the hill to see a bear coming up towards him. He quickly climbed a tall, sturdy tree and the bear came up and began trying to shake him out of it. After a few minutes the bear gave up and retreated down the hill. Ten minutes passed and Jim climbed out of the tree only to hear more noises coming from the direction of the bear. He peered over the hill and saw the first bear returning with a partner. Up the tree he went again as both bears began shaking the tree trying to dislodge him. After a few minutes they gave up and disappeared as before. Jim didn't wait for a repeat performance and quickly left the area.

Some time later a warden patrolling the area had a similar experience. Noises alerted him to a bear's presence and he climbed a tree which the bear shook violently for a few minutes before giving up and disappearing down the hill. Ten or fifteen minutes passed and the warden climbed down and cautiously approached the edge of the hill to see if he could see the bear. At the bottom of the hill he saw the animal approaching for another attempt, only this time, following behind the bear waddled a beaver.

THE STUDENT BEAR

Jim Deegan

ORKY was the bull cook at Mount Coleman Camp #3 at Mile 102 on the Banff-Jasper Highway, circa 1950. One of his jobs was splitting firewood and hauling it to the cookhouse in a wheelbarrow. But, unbeknownst to him, Yorky had an audience for his labours.

A great black bear sat on his haunches beside the warehouse, which incidentally, housed the food cooler. This bear was studying every move that Yorky made.

The bear noticed the way Yorky carried the firewood: his left arm extended at a 90° angle from his body, hand upturned and curled so as to accept the armful of wood. The bear was fascinated with how Yorky opened the door to One-Eyed John's cookhouse with his right hand.

This bear had ulterior motives … and he made his move. Wheeling about, he grasped the door handle latch and with a heave flung the six-inch thick door wide open—rows of sausages and wieners, crates of eggs, cartons of butter, slabs of bacon and pails of lard, jam and honey were revealed.

Standing upright with his left front leg extended and paw curled, he selected his booty with his right meat-hook, claws delicately grasping their booty. Balanced like an experienced waiter, the bear shuffled out of that food cooler with enough grub to last a company of soldiers for a week.

But in politeness he closed the door firmly, then ambled across the river to dine at his leisure.

VI

TERROR ON THE TRAIL

Stories of Tragedy and Survival

INCIDENT AT SPRAY LAKE

Dan McCowan

The earliest recorded fatality by bear attack in the mountain parks occurred in 1914 near a logging camp on Spray Lake. It remains one of the most bizarre bear-attack stories.

*T*HERE is no more awesome creature than a wounded grizzly bear and, save the wild goat perhaps, no animal more tenacious of life. As illustrative of this I cite the incident of the Spray Lake grizzly and the manner of his passing.

Some years ago two men employed by the Eau Claire Lumber Company were at work on a timber limit near Spray Lakes about twenty five miles south of Banff. They occupied a small log hut near the cabin of the Park Warden stationed in that district. A chum of the woodcutters decided that while on vacation he would visit his friends and thereupon walked from Canmore to the Lake arriving there late in the evening. The next morning he set off alone to fish. Some miles from the hut he saw at a distance a grizzly bear tearing a fallen log to pieces, and at once retreated thinking of a rifle and a bearskin rug. At noon he told his friends about the bear and asked for the rifle which he knew they had concealed in a hollow log, and for some of the ammunition, which was hidden in a syrup can hanging under the ridgepole of the hut, supposedly to catch a rain drip. The Warden had previously asked the men if they possessed any guns or ammunition but was told that they knew Park regulations too well to risk being caught with an unsealed weapon. The woodsmen gave their friend the rifle, warning him to be wary both of the warden who was out on patrol, and of the bear. Laughing at their timidity he swung along the trail by the edge of the lake. Presently he again sighted the busy animal grubbing amongst the rotten pine logs, and having an easy target felled the unsuspecting victim with two well placed bullets. Approaching the stricken bear he fired two more shots into the body and pressed his heel into the ribs to satisfy himself that the creature was actually dead.

Hurrying back to where the lumbermen were at work he told them of his kill and asked them to accompany him to skin the beast and hide the carcass before the Warden should discover it. When the three men reached the place where the animal had supposedly been slain the body had disappeared. There was a spattering of blood on the stones and kinnikinik leaves, and a red spot or two on the ground led them to search for the victim, knowing that he must be grievously hurt and in all probability disabled beyond resistance. Walking abreast some few paces apart, with the hunter in the middle position, they scouted through some fallen timber with here and there a small lodgepole pine standing erect. Quick as a flash and with a hoarse growl the bear, all blood and froth, leaped over a log behind which it had lain to rest and ignoring the men on either side, made straight for the one with the rifle. He dropped to one knee and aimed steadily, waiting until the maddened brute was but a few feet away and then pressed the trigger. Instead of a flash and the loud bang of explosion there was a feeble click—the rifle missed fire. With but one blow of a forepaw the raging animal broke the hunter's neck killing him instantly. The others ran in terror and reaching the cabin, telephoned news of the tragedy to Banff. Close to the body of the hunter the search party found the bear, stark in death. It was a small grizzly about three years old, but it had a great heart and died like a veteran. Chief Warden Sibbald would fain have had the animal mounted and displayed in the Park's Museum, not as a warning to poachers in a wild life sanctuary, but as a tribute to the fortitude and endurance of a fine animal.

THE LONELY STRUGGLE
OF TOM BEDELL

Lukin Johnston

No one was present during the final moments of trapper Tom Bedell's life, but evidence left at the scene of his death provided enough information for author Lukin Johnston to recreate his desperate battle with a grizzly bear in a remote valley of the northern Rockies during the early spring of 1926.

TWOJACKS Creek is a tributary of the McGregor River which empties into the mighty Fraser, some forty miles north-east of Giscome Portage. In early June it is a rushing torrent, fordable, but dangerous to man and beast, for the swiftness of the muddy waters carries sizable rocks downward helter-skelter. By late September Twojacks Creek is a dried-up, stony watercourse. From November on through the long Winter till early Spring a trickle of water runs onward beneath the feet-thick crust of snow. But there are places here and there where the icy covering can be broken through, and thither come the creatures of the wild—the grizzly, the great antlered moose, the dreaded timber wolf—to slake their thirst. Half a mile on, the creek widens out into a small lake a few acres in extent but very deep, and at the outlet the hard-working beaver are wont to build a dam.

The course of Twojacks Creek, in short, is such as an experienced trapper would choose for his location.

In November 1925 came Jean Ledoux, French-Canadian, and Tom Bedell, trappers, and established their tented winter quarters on the edge of a natural clearing in the forest, back two hundred yards from the course of the creek. They collected dry wood against the perishing cold to come, banked up the tents and made all snug. Half a hundred traps the partners set out when the snow came—a score or more along the creek-bed and others near the outlet of the lake.

By late March, though the fur harvest had not been good, furs of many kinds—beaver, marten, fisher and fox—were "cached" in the boughs of near-by trees or stretched on frames outside the tent.

On the morning of March 24th Bedell prepared to visit some traps he had set out three days before in a south-easterly direction from the camp.

"Grub's gettin' low, Tom," said Ledoux as his partner lashed his snowshoes to his feet. "Mebbe you better bring back a piece of de moose you kill las' week near de lak."

"All right, Jean, I'll take the axe along with me, and leave the rifle at home," said Bedell. "I'll be back before noon."

He set out along the well-worn trail, his figure swathed in heavy mackinaw and felt puttees, and his two-and-a-half-pound axe stuck in his girdle. Ledoux watched from the cabin door until the stooping figure, with its swinging, steady gait, was out of sight round a bend in the trail.

Spring was coming early this year, but the layer of melting snow on the top had frozen in the night and snowshoeing was hard going. Half a mile down the trail, Bedell stopped and, unlashing his snowshoes, hung them in a tree and proceeded over the hard crust in his moccasined feet.

On his return journey he was making his way to the carcass of the moose down by the lake-shore. The trail was only just wide enough for men in single file and on either side the dense forest closed in, where the snow lay four feet deep. A few yards ahead of him was a trail branching off to the lake.

As the trapper came abreast the turning and wheeled to the left, there, ten yards in front of him, was a grizzly. Its immense body blocked the whole width of the trail.

Hesitating momentarily, the huge beast gave forth a snarl of rage, calculated to strike terror to the stoutest heart. Then, dashing forward until he was within striking distance of the trapper, the monarch of the forest took up his position for battle—feet planted firmly, his whole body tense, head lowered and swaying menacingly this way and that like a pendulum, eyes watching his victim's every move. As he snarled viciously in his rage he bared cruel fangs.

For Bedell there was no escape. He was unarmed save for his puny axe, for who would expect a grizzly to be awake from his winter sleep so early in the year? The trapper could not run over the caked and slippery snow. The forest walls barred escape on either side. To give ground meant certain death. His only chance—one in a million at that—was to stand his ground and strike at the grizzly's eyes with his axe.

Disturbed at his meal on the moose carcass, the bear was in no mood to give quarter. He sprang at Bedell with a swiftness marvellous for an animal of his bulk. Hot saliva dripped from his jaws and spattered the trapper as the beast bellowed and roared in his rage.

With his left arm raised in futile defence of his head, Bedell swung his axe. The bear parried the blow, but it partly severed three claws of the left fore-paw. With a howl of pain the grizzly lunged at his adversary with his right fore-paw. Again Bedell tried to parry the blow—but his left forearm was broken and fell limp at his side.

Mad with pain and seeing his end was near, one arm useless and blood streaming from a claw wound in his right hand, the trapper swung again with the axe and caught the bear a glancing blow on the shoulder. But his time was come.

The mighty right paw was raised again and swung like lightning to the trapper's head, smashing the skull and tearing the features from the luckless man's head. As the body fell, the grizzly, in a frenzy, rained a hurricane of blows on it, crushing the ribs and clawing the head into an unrecognisable ghastly pulp of human flesh.

So Tom Bedell died.

His partner, alarmed at his failure to return at nightfall, set out next day to look for him. He came first on the snowshoes, hung in the tree. Sensing disaster, he pushed on and came on the body lying face downward in the snow. Evidently the bear after his victory, had jumped on the body, pounding it into the hard crush of snow. Study of the tracks showed that the grizzly apparently had first fled from the scene and then had twice returned to the spot. A clean print of the hind-foot measured fourteen inches long by eleven inches wide. Three inside claws of the left foot were missing, leading to the belief that the bear had torn away the claws which Bedell's first blow had almost severed.

Leaving the body, Jean Ledoux trekked three days to the nearest police-post. The police report showed Bedell's effects to consist of one marble match safe, a bone-handled knife, a two-dollar watch and a Roman Catholic rosary and scapular. His only other asset was a one-third share in the winter's meagre catch of furs.

Sewing the body in canvas, they buried it, and over the spot erected a wooden cross inscribed: "Here is laid to rest Tom Bedell, killed by a grizzly bear, March 24th, 1926."

THE DEATH OF A WARDEN

Howard O'Hagan

The fatal grizzly attack on Warden Percy Goodair in Jasper Park's Tonquin Valley in September 1929, stands as one of the legendary tales of the Park Warden Service. Goodair was the first park warden killed in the line of duty. It was a curious coincidence that one of the Rockies' most respected writers, Howard O'Hagan, was in the party that uncovered the tragedy.

ONE sunny late-September afternoon long ago I stepped down from the westbound passenger at Jasper, Alta. I had come home for a three-week holiday from my job as publicity man for the Canadian National Railways in New York City. In the course of the holiday I was to enter a cabin just below timber-line and see before me the meagre tokens of existence left behind by a man who had gone out from its door on an errand of a few minutes and whose fate it was never to return.

At the Jasper station to meet me was Major Fred Brewster.

After shaking hands his first words were, "I've got the horses lined up and a cook and a horse-wrangler. Where would you like to go?"

The invitation was a surprise. Taking into account my two-way journey across the country and a day or two with my people, I would have no more than ten days to give to an expedition into the mountains.

I looked up the Athabaska Valley to Mount Edith Cavell, described by an early traveller as "a white sheet let down from the sky," and westward from there to Whistler mountain rising above the town, its blue slopes splashed with the vivid yellow of turned popular leaves. A day's travel by trail beyond Whistler was the Tonquin Valley where grim, ice-encrusted peaks lifted above the alpine meadows:

Turning to Brewster I told him that I would like to find a pass from

the Tonquin in Alberta over into the Fitzwilliam Basin in British
Columbia. Years before when I lived in Lucerne on Yellowhead Lake I
had often hiked up a trapper's trail into the Fitzwilliam Basin, a place of
muskeg and spruce drained by a deep and slow-moving stream. In those
days I had still to see the Tonquin. I knew it lay beyond the ridges to
the south but I had not found the way across to it.

In later years, working as a guide for Brewster I had often taken
horses into it from Jasper. The pilgrims I guided however invariably
had to return to the railroad within a prescribed number of days and
there was never time to discover if a route passable for horses existed
between the Tonquin and Fitzwilliam basin.

Now for the first time and with a full outfit at my disposal I was to
have the part of a pilgrim. Brewster, stocky, rocky, with a clipped brown
moustache and a leathery complexion, a man then in his forties, was
one of the "Brewster Boys," six or seven of them, who since the turn of
the century had been guides out of Banff and later out of Jasper. Fred,
with his younger brother, Jack, had come into the Athabaska Valley
before the laying of steel around 1908.

Charlie Bowlen, our horse-wrangler, was the son of a pioneer Alberta
rancher and one of Brewster's top hands. Tall, slow-spoken, he was an
outstanding horseman. Our cook was Joe Weiss, a German-Swiss.

Two mornings after my arrival in Jasper, Brewster and I were driven
ten miles up the highway to Portal Creek. There at the bridge the outfit,
saddled and with the packs ready to be thrown on, waited for us. Alec
Nelles, a Jasper Park warden, was there too. He was to travel with us as
far as the ranger's cabin in the Tonquin. We pulled out, a string of five
saddle-horses and five carrying packs. Following Portal Creek to its head
we would cross Maccarib Pass and from it drop down into the Tonquin.

By lunch-time we were in snow and later on in the pass it lay two feet
deep, gleaming against the sun until it seemed to blister the eyes. Crossing
the pass, Mount Geikie, the Ramparts and other peaks above the Tonquin
came into view, white-robed, majestic, like a vision of frozen eternity.

About five o'clock in the afternoon Brewster, Ellis and I dismounted
before the ranger's cabin. Bowlen and Weiss went on with the rest of
the outfit to make camp a mile or so farther down the valley.

The warden in the Tonquin was a man named Goodair. An Englishman with a taste for literature, especially for the works of Robert Louis Stevenson, he was thought to be a veteran of the Klondyke gold rush. Like many men in that country who chose to spend most of their days alone, he was reticent about his past. I had last seen him a couple of years before loading a pack-horse in the government corral in Jasper. Pulling tight the final hitch of his "diamond" he did not, as most men do, put his foot against the pack. Instead, holding a longer length of rope in hand, he stood off and tugged from a distance as though he feared to go close to the horse's hooves.

Coming down the trail we had remarked that no smoke showed from his cabin chimney. He might well have been out looking after his horses but now, with dusk approaching, we thought that he would soon be returning.

Here a thousand feet below Maccarib Pass the snow was only inches deep in the stunted timber. The snow was a recent fall from the usual equinoctial storm and in a few days most of it would disappear to be followed by two or three weeks of "Indian Summer."

Approaching the cabin and seeing no footprints leading to its door we decided that Goodair was absent with his horses on a patrol of the park's western boundary—until we observed his saddle-gear and panniers laid out on the porch protected under the over-hang of the roof.

We tied our horses to the nearby hitching rail, unlatched the cabin door and knocking the snow from our boots, went inside. It was hushed, chill and in twilight. The plank-topped table was set with knife, fork, spoon and enamel cup. Against the west wall, the bunk with its crimson Hudson's Bay blanket was neatly made, a grey mackinaw shirt tossed upon it. By the stove the wood-box was full. On the cold stove was the making of a meal, bacon and potatoes partly cooked.

Brewster went over to the bunk and lit a match to see the time upon the watch hung by its leather strap from a nail in the log wall. The watch was stopped at 20 minutes after six. It might have stopped that morning or the night before. Snow had been falling on the mountains around Jasper for the two days previous to our departure. Goodair had set out from his cabin before that time because he left no footprints

141

behind him. He had been absent now for at least two days and two nights when all the indications—the half-cooked food, the set table—showed that he had intended to be away only a matter of minutes.

What had called him from his preparations for a meal we could only guess. Perhaps a passing horse's bell, and he had gone out to see that all of his several horses were on hand. But that had been two days or more ago and the timber-line Tonquin Valley was prime grizzly country.

A single strand of wire strung upon the trees led down Meadow Creek to the railroad and connected the telephone on the cabin wall with the park headquarters in Jasper. Nellis·went to the telephone and twisting the handle rang the combination which put him through to the chief warden ... Dick Langford.

"There's something wrong up here," Nellis said into the mouthpiece and then described the circumstances of our arrival at Goodair's cabin. Langford set out early the next morning on the 30-mile ride from Jasper reaching the Tonquin that afternoon.

He has recently told me of the thoughts that came to him upon receiving Nellis' message. He remembered that ten days earlier Goodair had called for permission to make a four-day patrol south to the head of the Whirlpool. He believed that trappers from B.C. were setting themselves up there for a winter's illegal trapping in Jasper Park. Langford advised him to "go ahead."

The first thing that Langford noticed as he approached the cabin the afternoon following Nellis' call was that Goodair's saddles, blankets and panniers were neatly arranged under the over-hang of his porch. He had completed his arrangements for the patrol. His next logical step would have been to go out and bring in his horses or at least, if this was on the evening before his planned departure, to go out and discover where they were so as to make their finding easier in the morning.

Langford knew, as we did not, that to this end Goodair had a favoured "look-out" a few hundred yards behind and above his cabin from which he could scan the sparsely timbered valley-floor. Leaving his horse, Langford at once began the short climb to the look-out.

Not much more than a hundred yards from the cabin, he came upon Goodair's snow-covered body, just beyond a piece of down-timber which spanned the faint trace of trail. Mackinaw shirt and flesh were torn from one side of the dead man's chest, the ribs caved in. Before dying Goodair had used his bandana handkerchief in an effort to staunch the flow of blood from his mortal wound.

Several times the previous summer he had written in his diary—a record which all park wardens keep—of sighting a grizzly bear and her yearling cub close to his cabin. In the park grizzlies, like other animals, are protected and in any case if unmolested are seldom a threat to man.

Langford now believes that immediately after his telephone conversation with Goodair of ten days before the latter, having gathered his gear together, interrupted his supper-making for a final glance at his horses' where-abouts. On his way up to the look-out he jumped over the down-timber across the trail and landed where the she-grizzly was bedded down with her cub. Broken branches on a nearby 30-foot spruce tree indicated that he had tried to escape her assault by climbing it. Reports to the contrary notwithstanding, grown grizzlies with their long straight claws, unlike the smaller black bears with their curved ones, do not climb trees.

Goodair was buried two days later in a coffin which Langford and Nellis made from the whip-sawed lumber of the cabin's porch. The simple ceremony was attended by members of the Masonic Order who rode in from Jasper. With them were Tony Frere, Inspector of the RCMP, and my father, Thomas O'Hagan, the town doctor, who was there as coroner.

Goodair's grave is on a bluff behind his cabin and to this day is carefully tended by the park authorities. On its head-piece are inscribed a few lines from Stevenson's "Requiem."

"Home is the sailor, home from the sea
And the hunter, home from the hill."

This column was to have been a chronicle of finding a new pass across the mountains, from Alberta into B.C. Instead it has become that of one man's last minutes on earth as he made ready to go on with his duties for another day. It has been truly said, "A man dies, but his name lives on."

AT GRIPS WITH A GRIZZLY

Nick Morant

as told to Colin Wyatt

The following account details a grizzly attack on the CPR photographer Nick Morant and Swiss guide Christian Häsler, which took place in Yoho Park on 19 September 1939. While one can admire Nick's feisty spirit in the face of danger, he violated nearly every rule of what to do when attacked by a bear. He was lucky to survive.

CHRISTIAN Häsler and I had gone out to take some pictures; we left from near Field at 6:30 in the morning, went up from Sherbrooke Lake near Wapta Lake. Since we were in a national park we didn't carry a rifle. We followed the trail for quite a way and we had got up above the far end of the lake near the tree line when we came on a grizzly with her cub. As we saw her she looked up at us very casual-like and Häsler said to me: "Look at that big grizzly over there!" I looked up and saw her and wasn't very worried, for I had met them before and they had never bothered me.

Häsler said: "We'll have to wait and let her make up her mind what she's going to do." She was right in the trail—so we waited and the old bear turned to her cub and they went across the creek and up toward Mt. Ogden.

Well, I figured, she'll mind her own business. She'll go her way and we'll go ours. But that's where we made our mistake—we should never have trusted her.

After we had gone along a little we looked back and there was the cub up on the mountain all by himself and no mother grizzly—then the next moment we looked over our shoulders to our left and there was mother grizzly coming after us as hard as she could come. Boy! Was she traveling!

Häsler and I threw off our rucksacks with our heavy equipment and we ran as hard as we darned well could up into the trees. Now you just go out one afternoon when you've nothing else to do and try and run up a tree as if a grizzly was after you. You've got to be up fifteen feet in fifteen seconds, and it's not very easy—go out and try some day! That's what we had to do.

I figured to myself that the first man to climb a tree would be the first man to get caught and if I ran further than Häsler then maybe I'd be in the clear. So that's what I did. It's not a very Christian way of thinking, perhaps, but sometimes you forget about other people and start thinking about yourself. So I ran beyond Häsler as he started up a tree—when I climbed my tree and looked back there were his legs disappearing up into the branches and, almost at the same moment, the grizzly appeared at the bottom of his tree.

She looked so small, you know, it didn't look as if she'd ever be able to get him; his legs were 'way too high. But there I was wrong. I realized then something I'd never realized before, that a bear is just like a caterpillar—you know the way a caterpillar stretches itself right out? Well, a bear does the same thing. She stood up and she took him by the leg at nine feet from the ground. She grabbed him and ripped him right out of that tree, then she jumped on him and started to tear at him.

Poor Häsler was crying for help and there was I up my tree and not knowing what to do. Now if you were up a tree and saw a friend being torn by a grizzly, what would you do? There's a real predicament; would you stay up in the tree or would you come down and try and help the other one? I really didn't know what to do, because sometimes in the bush the glorious thing to do isn't the smart thing. Maybe it's better for me to stay up here, I thought, and then, when the bear's finished mauling him, there will be someone to look after him and get help; but, on the other hand, in the meantime he's being killed. So I had quite a decision to make, for a grizzly is pretty big and you haven't much chance of coming out of it alive.

Anyway, I came down out of the tree, up behind the old grizzly, and whacked her over the backside with a stick. The grizzly didn't like that very much. She swung around and she came at me and I started to run.

145

I was heading for Banff! Then I remembered that a grizzly can move awful fast—it can overtake a horse in an open field. So I knew if she came up behind me she would strike at me with her paws—and if you look at those rugs you'll see the size of a grizzly's paws, the claws are as big as Eversharp pencils. When a grizzly swipes at you with those claws it's like someone sticking daggers into you; just cuts you all to pieces or knocks your head off.

So I threw myself on the ground so that the bear wouldn't have a chance to strike at me with her claws and when she rushed me I kicked her in the face with my big boots.

Well, when I kicked her she got very mad. She was just as quick as lightning and grabbed my leg in her mouth. Do you feel that? Put your finger in that hole in my leg. It comes clean through the other side. The leg was split in half, just like that, quick as it takes to tell it. See the muscles here? That's where they broke through the casing. The leg was broken in two places and the muscles ripped through.

When I found the grizzly had my leg in her mouth I was very scared. I beat at her with my fists to make her let go. She let go, but then she grabbed me by the arm—see here, a cut which showed all the muscles in my arm. That rendered my arm useless and my leg useless. Then, just as quickly as she'd attacked me, she went back after the still-unconscious Häsler.

I had to get up and try to get away, but I found I had a leg broken in two places and a bad arm. I thought I'd climb a tree, but I couldn't even do that. So I just leaned against a tree. You have to remember that when you are in an accident like that, there's what the doctors call shock; you're terribly weak, you're terribly scared, you're like a little boy.

So I stood there, leaning against a tree, and, having mauled Häsler again, she came back looking for me.

Now remember that a grizzly's sight is not very good, and that I had figured the first person to climb a tree would be the first person she'd see. Well, this time she came rushing past within two feet of me—she never saw me but went rushing headlong by me. I could have touched her with my hand as she went past. She stopped about ten feet beyond me, swung around, and came back on the other side of the tree. She stood there with her behind to me and I could have reached round and touched her.

Then she must have smelled the blood on me—or more likely she must have heard me breathing, for I was breathing very heavily. So she whips around the tree and comes at me with a hell of a roar and down I go and bite the dust again.

When she came back at me I swiped at her with my other arm and she grabbed me up here at the upper part of the elbow—she grabbed me and shook me like a rat. Have you ever seen a puppy shake a rag doll? Then she threw me about ten or fifteen feet—it felt like farther—and I landed face down in a bunch of rocks. I lay there and felt pretty sick.

Now, while all this was happening, Häsler regained consciousness and realized there was nothing he could do as he was pretty badly wounded—his arm was terribly hurt and all the muscles of his leg were exposed down to the shinbone. He made a run for it and got away. He ran and walked, and fell unconscious about eight times, all the way back to Wapta Lake. But I didn't know that, you remember, I didn't know he'd got away.

So, after the bear had finished with me and thrown me in the rocks face down, she went back to look for Häsler. But she couldn't find him. She went rushing around in the bush looking for him and I just lay there. I could see her running around. She was so big that when she hit a tree the whole tree would shake.

I lay there and wondered what would happen—I really didn't care too much. Anyway, suddenly she came out of the brush and she makes a rush for me again. She came right at my face so I roll over and turn my face down into the rocks. She bit me all over my body—she took me behind the ear and just lifted all the side of my scalp right up ... (I remember everything very well; I didn't get unconscious or anything like that—at least, I don't think I did.)

Then she stepped on me once, just like somebody putting a grand piano on me, a terrible weight. She walked right clean over me and past me, over to where the trail was.

I looked up and there was the cub; he'd come down from the mountainside. That cub saved my life.

But I was very annoyed, for I always believed that if you left animals alone they'd leave you alone—and so they will, except for the grizzly who is very unpredictable.

I swore at Mother Bear, called her every name under the sun; told her to go home.

And then she started at me a fourth time. Just as she came at me the cub let out a little yelping noise, she turned around and went off down the trail with the cub.

Now you may think that's the end of the story, but it isn't. It took Häsler about six hours to get out—he didn't get down until late afternoon.

Now you must remember that the bear went off down the trail between me and civilization and left me blocked up in a canyon. But I believed that Häsler was still there; but he wasn't, he was on his way out. So I figured I'd have to go and get help. I worried about him so I went to look for him as best I could with a broken leg in two places. I couldn't find him, so there was only one thing to do and that was to go and get help, and, to get help I had to go out behind the bear; if I went down the trail I'd run into the bear again.

There was only one thing to do and that was to circle the area; in other words go all around where I thought the bear was. The mountains there are very steep and I had to go and look for a way out. I had to cross the creek, and I marked my trail with my windbreaker so they would know where to look when they came looking for Häsler.

I climbed nearly two thousand feet up Mt. Ogden with my broken leg, right up to the snow line, walked all day and climbed down to the shores of Sherbrooke Lake, and there I found the people going out to look for me. I had been eleven hours out with no help at all—the blood was clotted three inches deep on my shoulder, and the first man I met fainted at the sight of me. I had a very bad time of it.

Both Häsler and I lived to tell the story, but he died a year or two later from a heart attack. I was in hospital a long time, but I've now completely recovered.

HIT-AND-RUN

Harry Rowed

After many years of roaming the trails of the Canadian Rockies, one of Jasper's best-known professional photographers and his wife ran afoul of a pair of grizzly bears on 1 September 1972. This attack was highly unusual in that two bears were actively involved.

*H*AVE you ever been threatened by a ferocious dog, snarling and ready to attack on slightest pretext?

All right, let's multiply his weight and size by anything up to ten times. Now you have a 400-pound grizzly charging, jaws agape, his speed probably close to 30 miles an hour.

That's what happened to the two of us, a grizzly each, one fine September morning near Jasper.

Many Skyline Hikers know Valley of the Five Lakes. It is a succession of rocky ridges and elongated lakes, eight miles south of Jasper. During the summers, dozens of hikers and fishermen walk to the chain of lakes from which the name is derived. Old pack trails feel their way along the ridges, trails which have provided exercise and deep pleasure for Gen and me and our children.

On this September morning we parked along the highway just before 11 o'clock. This was to be a short hike, lunch near one of the lakes, the walk out by mid-afternoon. The packs were light—lunch, thermos, jackets and camera.

With a quarter-century of hiking behind us precautions have become habit. Grizzlies are never far from thought when hiking in the Canadian Rockies. We often use noise-makers, either hanging bells from the packs or periodically jingling a can and pebbles. Following the habit of years, I slung my camera over my shoulder before hoisting the pack so there'd be no conflict of straps if the pack had to come off in a hurry. The waist strap hung loose for the same reason.

There was no premonition of danger. We knew at once the feeling of well-being which pervades almost from first steps on a mountain trail.

Some animal signs were noticeable in the dust of the trail ... deer tracks, elk droppings. But no sign of the deep claw marks of the grizzly, although meagre droppings of a bear did appear where bear berries were plentiful. "A small black, probably," Gen commented. But the can and pebble jangling took on added frequency.

A few hundred yards from the highway the trail drops a few feet to cross a creek, then traverses to the left for ascent of the first ridge. So the legs would gear down a little, the breathing become deeper. We would stop at the top and look back for the view of Mount Edith Cavell.

That was the end of the pleasant reverie.

A succession of heavy grunts and snorts, the crash of big animals bouncing through underbrush and trees, and two grizzlies broke into the small clearing. They bore down on us like a couple of tanks, on all fours and at full speed, the bellows of anger, the terrifying *whuffs*.

For years I had envisaged an attack by a charging grizzly. Stand your ground. Get the pack out front. We crashed together at my left shoulder, a frightening mismatch.

All I recall is being bowled over and over. Assessment of damage came later. The pack and camera took the brunt. Back slats of the pack were bitten in two, the metal hip rests twisted like pretzels. A heavy thermos was reduced to splinters of glass and metal. Somehow the tough Leica SL got into the line of attack. Camera and pack took bites which would have ruined me. Had the bear's rage hit home my head and shoulders would have been crushed between powerful jaws.

Gen's thought: "How badly will we be mauled?" She dodged nimbly as her bear zeroed in through an obstacle course of shrubs and trees. She saw me go down, moved to help. Her bear, furious, moved in to disembowel her, the classic attack of animals of prey. She pushed her arms into the deep fur of his hump and bent over as he bit into her stomach. She screamed.

"Down on your stomach. Put your arms over your head." The bear sniffed at her back. Then they were gone, a real hit and run attack. We stayed prone for perhaps a minute, fearing their return. Should we climb trees? Or head for the car? Gen was hurt and bleeding; there was only the latter choice.

We were incredibly lucky. Gen's stomach gash missed disemboweling her by a fraction of an inch, a near brush with death.

Our wounds were almost insignificant when we think of friends who have been "hit" by grizzlies. Our tangle with the big bears turned out to be least damaging of any we know, except perhaps psychologically. Even now, several years later, we sometimes awake in a cold sweat after having fought off grizzlies in a bad dream.

PLAY DEAD!

Lorne Perry

During the summer of 1990, Calgary artist-designer Lorne Perry was hiking alone near the headwaters of Tokumm Creek in Kootenay Park when he experienced every hiker's worst nightmare—a sudden encounter with a sow grizzly and cubs at ten paces.

I'VE always been a little frightened of bears, grizzly bears in particular. They're on my mind now and again whenever I've been in the back country. But having had no serious incidents over many years of hiking and mountaineering I had begun to view my fears as a silly paranoia. Nothing serious. I had followed the huge, clawed tracks in the mud after a mountain storm, but very rarely encountered the real thing. The presence of the master in his domain was more felt than seen, and had become nothing to worry about. You might call me careless.

But a quiet three-day trip in the rugged highlands brought pain beyond what I thought I could endure; terror as dark and terrible as anything I could imagine; a moment of agony that I would never see the family I loved so dearly again. The struggle would bring me to my knees, high in a boulder strewn mountain pass, swaying unsteadily, watching my life drip away into the snow. I came within a tiny eternity of death. Call it bad luck that it happened, good luck that I survived, or simply fate.

My intention was to use the August long weekend to do a solo hiking, climbing, and sketching trip beginning from the Radium Highway. I planned to hike up to a steep pass, climb a peak the next day, then descend to my car in the spectacular Lake Moraine area. My pack was heavy—loaded with my camera, sketching materials, and climbing gear.

Late in the evening, 12 kilometres along the creek, the trail began climbing eastward and away from the valley floor. No problem, I was expecting that. But where was the other trail that would take me directly along the valley and up over the pass?

Some searching up and down the creek made it clear no such trail existed. That meant no one else would be around. I would be completely alone. The sun was setting and the forest seemed somehow colder and darker. I began to look over my shoulder.

I set out along the creek following a very old trail that was overgrown and frequently disappeared and re-appeared. It was low and boggy as I stepped over deadfall and into deep wet grass. Thin spider webs clung to my face. I moved steadily upstream and was in the middle of a small clearing when I was brought to an abrupt halt with a shock.

"Dammit ... dammit to hell!"

I stared at the huge mound of bear dung. This was not what I wanted to find. It was not fresh—maybe a couple of days old—but it was enough to set pictures of dark, powerful brutes with slashing teeth tearing their way into my nightmares.

Darkness began to spread its quiet, cool hand across the valley. High above, the clouds were touched with pink and orange—time to find a campsite. I set up my tent. The noisy little one-burner stove chuttered away, heating the evening meal. It had been a long day. Sleep came easily.

The sun was up. Inside the tent, already warmed, I could hear the creek and the birds in the meadow. Any nervousness over finding the bear sign the previous night evaporated with the morning dew.

I packed up quickly, going through the routine I have gone through many times before—everything exactly in its place. Little did I know that somewhere ahead in a clearing, waited a presence that would demand some quick decisions based on such previous knowledge.

The forest had begun to thin out, giving way to an occasional alpine meadow. But there were high willows along both sides of the creek. That's bad news because you can't see anything coming—and it can't see you. I mean bears.

Well aware of the dangers of a close encounter, that one chance in a million you've read about but can't happen to you, I began to clap and shout as I walked. It was nerve-wracking to think I actually was acknowledging, not just in thought but in actions now, that something might happen.

I walked into a clearing—and time stopped. There was a large dark form, slightly uphill and ten metres away … moving. My Christ, oh my God! A grizzly.

She was surprised, instantly enraged, and up on her hind legs. Something rose up from the pit of my stomach and filled my chest with constricting, total terror. Front legs off the ground, paws stretched, claws out, she snarled and snorted, swinging her great heavy head left and right. The cubs behind her halted and tumbled backwards. Then she was coming. Nothing would stop her. I knew she had me.

There was nowhere to run. An inner voice told me: "You are alone. You're finished." I felt my face grow huge as my mouth gaped. My ears told me I was screaming: "No. Noooooooo!" Everything was in slow motion that lasted forever.

I felt my body move a few steps backwards on legs that weren't mine and was aware of my hands coming up to protect myself. She came at me shifting slightly right, hesitated momentarily, dark jaws seized my wrist and teeth cut through flesh. Darkness.

I was toppling backwards down a hill. The maddened bear was somewhere near me, I knew. There was no pain as I slid sideways. "Where am I?" was the next thought. The shock of the cold water soaking my left side gave me a clue.

From somewhere came the frantic message: "PLAY DEAD, PLAY DEAD, PLAY DEAD." I could hear desperate panting—"Hah, Hah, Hah, Hah." Jaws clamped around my head, blood began to run down my temple. I heard a snort. My hands were up around my face and out the corner of my eye I saw a foot and claws on my shoulder. My elbows were a little above my body. I felt teeth cut through and heard the crunch like a dog dismembering a pork joint.

"No! Don't shout! Play dead, damn you, play dead." I didn't move. I was silent. She was silent. And then as quickly as she had come, she vanished up and over the bank looking for the cubs she had misplaced when we crashed down into the creek bottom.

I lay still on my side in the water. Then pain, unbelievable pain. And a one-man dialogue began ... "What happened? You've been attacked by a bear." I could hear myself sobbing. "No! None of that ... control, yes, that's it. If you don't play your cards right you might just die right here.

"Now where is that goddam bear?"

It was still quiet. I could see blood running in the water and knew things were serious. I got up on my knees and looked down at the sorry sight of my arms and hands.

"This can't be happening. Why me?"

I searched round with a crazy stare as if there should be someone to offer comfort. But there was no one.

My right forearm was oozing blood from my elbow down and it would not move. My wrist was the same covered with deep bleeding holes, already swollen stiff and black with dirt and coagulated blood. I saw my finger ugly, swollen—dislocated. I clenched my teeth, braced for the pain and with my other hand pulled the finger back in place.

Using my teeth and one good hand, I began to pull each item out of my pack, leaving a jumbled heap of gear on the rocks. I had to lighten the load, taking only the essentials for what would be a difficult, painful journey back. My mouth tasted peculiar and I spat red onto the rocks.

The clock was running and it was time to move. The bear might come roaring back at any second. And if I arrived too late in the day, any hikers would have gone home and I would be left to my blood and pain in the cold of an alpine night. Ice axe ready, I half crawled, half walked through the creek. At any moment I expected to feel the claws and be dragged backwards into the stream. Somehow I found myself up the other side and going.

The meadows were torn up all along the way where bears had been digging. Panic rose and had to be beaten back again and again. But after several hours, there was still no sign of her so I began to slow down. I simply put one foot in front of the other trying to gain the upper valley. The question? "Will there be people up at the pass?" I sank down in a patch of snow and with my forehead on the cool metal of my ice axe watched the drip, drip, drip of blood into the snow. I pushed on.

I raised my good arm as a shield against the sun. I squinted and stared. "Yes, Yes, Yes! Bodies ... I see people!" A figure was coming down the steep scree. Gord Hurlburt drew closer and soon was beside me. The world became sane. I knew I was safe. Home.

He was one of two geologists who came to my assistance and was well prepared with medical supplies. But what followed was not easy going. We reached the summit of the pass about four o'clock and continued on down to where helicopter pick-up would be safer. The wait was long and wracked with pain. I took another pain killer, ate and rocked gently back and forth.

At Mineral Springs Hospital in Banff I was told that the wounds had become infected and that the outcome from bite wounds is not a foregone conclusion. There was a five per cent chance that I could lose my arm, my drawing arm, the one I depended on for a living. I felt as if I had been thrown right back into the fight again and spent feverish nights praying that the odds were still with me.

After a transfer to Foothills Hospital, the battle to control the infection was finally won. The plastic surgeon felt I would lose no fine motor skills and would be back to painting and drawing soon. I had been one of the lucky ones.

I feel no animosity toward the bear. In fact quite the contrary. I am concerned for her and her cubs. Where will they find peace? I am grateful to her for administering only such force as was required to do the job. Even with her superhuman strength and ferocious reputation, she showed more restraint than humans often do.

I am happy that I did not have to look down the barrel of a smoking gun at an ugly, lifeless form, and then watch the cubs, probably too young to fend for themselves, disappear in terror into the forest. It doesn't matter whether it is animals, plants or men, we are all part of a vast family of living things on this planet. The loss of wildlife is a loss for each one of us and that includes the monarch of the high country—the grizzly.

VII
IN THE LINE OF DUTY
Managing Bears in the Parks

TO WHOM IT MAY CONCERN

from the files

of the Jasper Park Superintendent, 1916 – 1931

To: J.B. Harkin, Commissioner, National Parks of Canada, Ottawa
From: Colonel Maynard Rogers, Superintendent, Jasper Park, 4 July 1916

Sir,

I have to report the necessity of shooting a bear here on Friday last. This animal, 2 – 3 yr old Black, had practically taken possession of the old Internment Camp, had gone in to the Staff Officers Store house and disputed possession with him on several occasions, had held up people coming off the bridges near there, and finally wound up by stampeding one of our best riding horses in through the barbed wire fence surrounding the stockade. He went clear through the barbed wire, into the stockade giving himself some eighteen to twenty cuts, and I thought it was about time to put Master Bruin out of business.

While on this subject I might mention that the Townsite has been overrun with bears this year, as many as six being counted at one time in the vicinity of the corrals, and I am afraid they cause a certain amount of nervousness amongst the women folk with small children ... I trust that the Berry season will lessen the trouble which at present is so very prevalent.

Yours faithfully,

To: A. Driscoll, Acting Superintendent, Jasper Park
From: Warden W.E. Biggs, 13 September 1916

Dear Sir,

I have had about ten complaints in the last few days about bears breaking into outside store rooms and carrying away provisions. There has been three cases of this in the last two days.

There is four bear in town and are seen every day. Women and children are afraid to go out of their homes and the children are afraid to go to school.

We have made coal oil torches and tried to drive them away but they go only as far as we go and then come back again. We also tried dogs and they go up a tree and come back when the dogs get tired barking.

I would like to be advised what to do as I am afraid they will pick up some child.

Yours truly,

To: A. Driscoll, Acting Superintendent, Jasper Park
From: J.B. Harkin, Commissioner, National Parks of Canada, Ottawa,
       19 October 1916

Dear Sir,

I beg to acknowledge the receipt of your letter of the 10th instant, your file 2.C. with regard to the question of the destruction of certain bears in Jasper Park which have been annoying the residents at certain points in the Park.

In this connection I beg to advise you that in a case where a particular bear becomes a real nuisance *you may authorize one of your Wardens to kill it*, but I would impress upon you that the case against the animal must be complete and that you must exercise the utmost judgement and discrimination.

You will readily understand that this branch is very much opposed to the destruction of any wild animals within the Park except under very exceptional circumstances, and I must rely upon you to deal with this question according to your best judgment on the ground.

Whenever the skin of a bear killed is of any value it should be carefully removed and disposed of in accordance with instructions from the Chief Superintendent.

Yours faithfully,

To: A. Driscoll, Acting Superintendent, Jasper Park
From: T.R. Buckham, Chief Warden, Jasper Park, 17 September 1917

Sir:

IN response to your request I went to Pocahontas and investigated the matter of a yearly bear being killed by a party of miners on Saturday the 15th and reported by Warden Biggs on Sunday the 16th.

I found that the bear was killed near the foot of the steps that are used to ascend the hill from the lower to the upper town about five o'clock Saturday.

The method of killing was apparently by stoning and clubbing the animal ...

I would recommend that action should be taken by you against such unwarranted and illegal conduct.

I am, Sir,

Your obedient servant,

To: *The Superintendent, Jasper Park*
From: *R. W. Langford, Supervising Warden, 27 September 1926*

Dear Sir:

*R*E bears at the Highways Camp—Jasper: It has been reported to me that bears have caused considerable damage to be done at this camp, and on Saturday last, Warden Davis killed a small black bear, which was supposed to be the chief offender. On Sunday afternoon some men from the camp notified Warden Davis they had two bears in a tree, and requested that he shoot them.

He immediately went to the scene and found the bears up a tree, situated half way up the hill at the back of the Camp, with a crowd of men and dogs at the bottom of the tree. As far as he could ascertain, these bears had not been at the Camp, and were just passing along the hill side. He instructed the people to go away from the tree and let the bears come down. After they went away, the bears came down and proceeded up the hill.

I went to the camp this morning, and found around the outside of the cesspit, which is quite close to the cook house door, a lot of old potato and carrot peelings, and smelling very badly. I instructed the cook to dig a hole at a suitable place into which to throw all his refuse, and to keep a fire burning in the hole. This was done last year by cook Tony at Cabin Creek, and they had no trouble with bears whatever, although there was as many around then as there is now.

As the bears around here are such an attraction for the tourists, if proper precautions are taken, they usually do not molest a camp. I therefore feel, that it is not necessary to shoot every bear seen in the vicinity of the Camp.

Yours faithfully,

To: *J.B. Harkin, Commissioner, National Parks of Canada, Ottawa*
From: *R.H. Knight, Acting Superintendent, Jasper Park, 15 September 1927*

Dear Sir:

RE bears: I beg to acknowledge receipt of your letter of September 3rd File u-212, in which you request an opinion as to the best method of dealing with the bear problem.

This has been very much in my mind during the past few months. When the bears were giving us the greatest trouble by disturbing campers, most of whom were Government employees, the people living in cottages at Lake Edith, and to some extent the people of Jasper, I was firmly convinced that some of the bears would have to be destroyed this fall. During the past three or four weeks, however, they have given very little trouble. Because of this and by reason that we need the bears as an attraction to the Park, I have changed my mind and have decided to spare the lives of these animals for the time being.

During the past Summer I have made special inquiry from tourists about bears in this and other Parks, and find that considerably more than half of them like to see the bears. I also learn from many of them that one of the chief attractions of the Yellowstone Park are the bears. During the past season it has been found necessary to kill about half a dozen of the animals because they were too bold and troublesome.

I respectfully recommend that no bears be killed in Jasper Park this fall, unless a limited number for some special purpose.

Next season I propose to carry on a vigorous campaign against feeding bears, and will also endeavour to limit their feeding grounds to two points, namely at the Lodge incinerator and the garbage dump for Jasper townsite. If this can be done I think the animals will be fairly under control. Another alternative which may be a possible solution of the bear problem for this Park is to place a bear proof fence around the garbage dump. In this fence there could be placed a trap gate that would not allow them to get out. In this way the bears would be under control and yet could be observed by the tourist.

About September 1st each year or some such suitable time they could be allowed their freedom. The fence would be so placed in the woods that it would not appear as an enclosure. This latter suggestion would be further investigated should my proposals for next year fail.

Yours faithfully,

To: *J.B. Harkin, Commissioner, National Parks of Canada*
From: *R.H. Knight, Superintendent, Jasper Park, 6 August 1931*

I beg to report that on August 1st Warden George Busby, while on patrol about half a mile North of the old mines at Miette, encountered a grizzly bear with a cub. Busby had a dog along with him which at first frightened the bear away and the cub climbed into a tree a short distance away. The mother bear apparently lost track of the cub and commenced running furiously around. After a few minutes it rushed towards Warden Busby, and when he thought he was in danger he fired two shots, but before he could fire a third time, the bear was within 15 feet of him, when it stopped and reared up on its hind legs. At this moment the dog appeared behind the bear who immediately took after the dog, whereupon Busby was able to make his escape. He is not certain that he hit the bear with either of the shots fired, but in any case the animal paid no attention to the report of the rifle. From Busby's statement I would gather that he had a very narrow escape.

Upon discussing the grizzly bear situation with him he states that during the month of July he has seen at least a dozen of these bears in the Athabaska Valley or on the hillsides near Miette. He accounts for their presence by the abundance of bear berries that are to be found in the locality, and considers they will remain in that vicinity until late in the fall.

During the past three or four months I have reported several cases of grizzly bears being seen close in, and I have reported this incident in order that you may be well in touch with the situation. It would seem that steps will have to be taken to reduce the number of these bears in Jasper Park, especially in the Athabaska Valley area. As an experiment, I would recommend that a couple of wardens be delegated to kill off half a dozen or so of these bears in the vicinity of Miette during the early part of September. It is thought that the fur will be prime by that time. As the hunting of these bears would entail considerable hard work as well as a certain amount of danger, I would further recommend that some bonus be allowed the wardens detailed to this work. Half the value of the hides might be a suitable consideration.

Yours faithfully,

THE FORGIVING WARDEN

Dan McCowan

*I*N the National Parks of Western Canada many wardens are employed, their business being to discourage poaching, to guard against forest fire and generally to promote the welfare of wild life within the sanctuaries. At one time these men were regarded, and rightly so, as gamekeepers whose activities were largely centred on the destruction of coyotes, hawks, weasels and other mammals and birds commonly classed as vermin. With official backing they waged total war on all things furred or feathered that did not come under the heading of "Game." Later, when it was decided that animals, other than those of vegetarian habit, had a rightful place in the Park areas, many wardens found it difficult to conform to changed conditions. To refrain from tracking down and destroying a cougar, to spare the life of a wolverine or to display a friendly attitude toward a lynx or badger—that was almost unthinkable.

This was, however, not so to Bill Hartley, who, amongst the many wardens I have met, was truly a friend and guardian to all birds and beasts within the area he patrolled. Bill was a Yorkshireman, a veteran of the first Great War, one of the type made immortal by Bairnsfather. When I first made his acquaintance he was stationed in Glacier National Park in British Columbia and had the entire sanctuary as his beat. He was then middle-aged and his gingery hair was thinning. But his eyes still had a merry twinkle and a slight wry twist to his mouth added further to the humorous cast of his countenance. Bill had but recently taken unto himself a wife and while the pair argued almost incessantly they were nevertheless extremely devoted to one another.

Possessed of a typical "tyke" dialect that none but Eric Knight could ever have put on paper, Bill's monologues on Natural History and

Current Events were a sheer delight. His attitude towards the creatures of the wild was revealed in an encounter with a bear that might well have cost him his life. He told me about it one afternoon as we sat and smoked in the lee of the woodshed, enjoying a breather after grinding a particularly dull and adamant axe. Shorn of picturesque speech and gesture the narrative was as follows.

During the previous summer a black bear loitering on the outskirts of the hamlet of Glacier by day and raiding larders at night had become a regular nuisance. One night it broke into the local general store and played havoc amongst the groceries. In the morning the wrathful storekeeper telephoned to Warden Hartley, whose station was distant about one mile, asking him to come at once and if possible hunt down and shoot the marauder. To this request Bill replied that he couldn't do that because as he phrased it, "I might kill the wrong bear." However, he said he would bring along a rifle and leave it in the store. Then, should the animal return for further pilfering amongst hams and honey, the storekeeper himself could take a shot at it. On the following morning at daybreak the hungry bear made its reappearance and was at once the target for several bullets. Staggering towards the river she collapsed on a gravel bar a short distance from the settlement.

At once the owner of the store notified Hartley that he had slain the shop-breaker and said that Bill had better come and skin the beast. So, after breakfast, William walked to the scene of the shooting and set about removing the pelt of the fallen animal. Standing beside the bear, the while sharpening his knife on a pocket whetstone, he inadvertently touched the sole of a hind paw with his boot. Immediately the supposedly dead creature sprang up and fiercely attacked the warden. Bill said, "She loomed right over me." He had set his rifle against a neighbouring tree and thus at the moment it was quite out of reach. The fight resolved itself into a rough-and-tumble scrap somewhat like a modern wrestling bout. The warden, although less than half the weight of his opponent, battled valiantly with fists and knife and feet and actually floored the animal two or three times. But she came at him again and again with what strength was left to her. Bill told me that although bitten and clawed repeatedly he did not fare too badly until the brute caught hold of his left hand with her teeth and severely crushed that member. He said, "When I heard the bones of my fingers cracking and crunching, I were vexed." By this time his adversary, weakened by wounds and loss of blood, became so enfeebled that Hartley was enabled to retrieve his gun and end the affray.

Bill spent many weeks in hospital at Golden as a result of the encounter but maintained that despite his injuries he bore no grudge against the luckless animal. As he said, with characteristic kindliness, "If I'd been in her place I'd have done just what she did."

SHOOT TO KILL

Frank Camp

Frank Camp grew up in Jasper, the son of a park warden. During World War II he witnessed the park's policy toward the hordes of black bears and grizzlies that invaded the town. Immediately following the war, he followed in his father's footsteps and joined the warden service. One of his first patrols was in the remote eastern wilderness of Jasper National Park, which had not seen a warden for several years. It was a tough life for the wardens; even tougher for the bears.

ONE of the greatest attractions when visiting the park was to see the bears, and very few people were disappointed. Garbage dumps were maintained at many resorts, and bears came to feed, giving visitors an excellent opportunity to observe and take pictures. First the black bears discovered this handout, but it wasn't long before the more cautious grizzly also frequented these feeding grounds, much to the delight of the visitor. Before bears discovered the succulent tid-bits of a garbage feeding station they considered man a danger, but as new generations of bears accepted handouts they took an offensive role and became dangerous.

Bear attacks on people became more frequent, and the Park had to take positive action. The first approach was to shoot the bear. When the Jasper Park Lodge closed for a few years during the war, the bears moved into the town of Jasper. At least 60 black bears were shot at this time by the wardens ...

I was sent to the Rocky River District with Jack Christiansen to shoot grizzlies. We were equipped with the 1895 Lee Enfield saddle carbine .303 and war surplus ammunition. The tips of the slugs had to be cut-off to keep the bullets from passing right through the animals. The decision to reduce the grizzly population was justified because for years the Rocky River district had been without a District Warden, and the bears had taken over the territory. Cabins had been ransacked, windows knocked out, and doors ripped off. The corners of the cabins were used as rubbing posts, and the bears had absolutely no fear of humans or horses.

On our first trip to the district, the snow was still on the trail, and we had to backpack the supplies we needed. Within a few days we had shot three grizzly on Osborne Creek and concluded it would be better to set a bait since there were still many tracks. Returning to town we obtained an old horse, bought more supplies, and returned to the Jacques Lake cabin. We shot the horse, then set a bait, secured to a large tree, in Osborne Creek and waited. We checked the bait frequently and soon had three more grizzly.

One morning a phone call over the forestry phone from a caretaker reported a grizzly trying to break into the Brewster chalet at Maligne Lake. I said I would go, and Jack stayed behind at Jacques Lake to watch the bait. That afternoon I hiked out to the Beaver cabin and caught a ride over the fire access road to Maligne. The next morning I crossed a grizzly track near the lake shore close to the chalet so I followed it into the Opal Hills. By mid-afternoon, following the timberline, I spotted the bear sunning himself beside a rock near a small patch of scrub alpine fir. There was very little cover to hide behind, but the wind was in my favour. I really didn't want to get too close in case my first shot didn't count and he could put the run on me. I finally was satisfied that I could get a good shot away and pulled down on him. I hit him behind the front shoulder, but the old army ammunition just wasn't enough to keep him down. Off he went into the small patch of alpine fir, and for about a half hour he thrashed about; then all was quiet. I sat around until dusk not daring to crawl into the brush but wanting to be sure he was finished.

I returned to Jacques Lake next morning and while Jack and I had lunch he told me about his experience during the night. The previous evening he had walked down to the creek and caught a couple of fair size dolly varden, cleaned them and hung them high on a pole in front of the cabin. He woke up during the night to the sound of two grizzlies standing on their hind legs fighting and trying to reach the fish. He opened the door and shot one, and the other took off. In the morning he got up at daylight to go and check the bait and had to step over the one lying dead in the yard. There was a black bear on the bait so he shot it and returned to the cabin for breakfast. To his surprise the bear he had stepped over in the morning was gone.

"Well at least after lunch we can go up to the bait and check out the black bear," he commented. To our surprise the black bear was also gone. By now we were a little concerned about what was going on, but after a search around the bait we found a trail going off into the bush. It looked as if something had been dragged. In about 300 yards a large circular area of ground had been pulled to the centre in a mound and buried underneath was the black bear. We knew for sure we had another grizzly around and increased our watch on the bait. There was a lot of speculation about the size of this unseen bear, and in a couple of days, when he paid us a visit, we were not disappointed. We watched as he came into view. When he approached the bait, we both shot and down he went. A couple of extra shots to the front legs ensured us he wouldn't go anywhere. Our instructions were to shoot and destroy as many bears as we found but not to save the hides. When we checked this one out he was a prime bear, 9 feet 3 inches from his nose to his tail, with an excellent pelt.

Without hesitation or a projected plan of what we could do with the hide, we skinned the bear. Packing it back to the cabin was hot and heavy work. It was mid-day and the warm spring sun was bringing out clouds of flies. We knew we had to flesh the hide, and the only place large enough to stretch it out was the back of the cabin. With some effort we lifted the nose to the ridge poles and securely nailed it. After the legs were spread and nailed we measured from the nose to the back pads; the distance was 11 feet 6 inches. We had no salt but were hoping if we kept fleshing all the fat and flesh off the hide it would dry properly. Unfortunately, the flies and hot weather got ahead of us and the pelt spoiled.

All was quiet on the bait for a few days so we decided to patrol on up the Rocky River to the Rocky Forks cabin. Our plan was to keep a lookout for more bears, and instead of travelling the regular trail down Jacques Creek and over the ridge to the Grizzly Cabin we went up Osborne Creek over Osborne Pass and returned to the Rocky River where the trail fords the river. There was still snow in the high country, and the stream we had to follow down to the main valley once we were across the pass was in flood. By the time we had come this far we were committed, and at every crossing we were nearly washed away. We crossed one at a time, and if we lost our footing the one on the bank was there to assist. We made it to the Grizzly Cabin, but before we could prepare supper we had to restore order to the place, which had been totally trashed by bears.

We got an early start the next morning and continued up the river, hoping the melt waters had receded during the night. We were concerned about crossing the Rocky River, which, under normal conditions, could be waded.

We made it to the Rocky Forks cabin that afternoon only to find that it had also been completely wrecked. No one had been to this cabin for years. Probably the last patrol was made by Dad in the early forties before he was transferred to the Whirlpool District. We had backpacked some supplies with us, enough for a couple of days. On our return trip we got to the river crossing, but found it in high flood. Our only choice was to go back to the cabin and wait.

By now we had used up our food supply and had to resort to salvaging some edibles the bears had left. A small cache of beans was still hanging from the ridge pole so we boiled and flavoured them with some crushed horse salt. There was a small amount of flour left in a tin, but mice had fouled it. An old window screen served as a sieve to separate most solids, and from this, mixed with water, we made a very flat pancake.

The river continued flooding so the plan was to go downstream about three miles below Stairway Falls and build a raft. We salvaged some telephone wire and found a few spikes, which we carried with us. Working our way down to the foot of the falls and looking at the river we decided we would never survive on the kind of raft we could build.

We cached the spikes and wire, which I'm sure to this day are still in the rock crevasse where we left them, and returned to the cabin.

While we waited around, without much food, we checked out some backwater springs below the mouth of the Medicine Tent River, looking for fish. The fish were spawning, hard to catch, and most unpalatable.

It was about 10 days before the river dropped and we could get back to Jacques Lake. Once back at the bait we shot two more grizzlies.

HAZARDOUS DUTY

Wilf Taylor with Alan Fry

Wilf Taylor was a warden in Banff and Yoho National Parks during the 1950s and early 1960s. In the course of his duties, he experienced many adventures and misadventures with bears.

WHEN a new warden station was under construction on the Panther River, a grizzly bear moved in to terrorize the work crew. The bear stole food, broke windows and generally made a mess around the camp.

I was sent to help Ed, another warden, deal with this bear, and we agreed that shooting the bear was the only choice.

We hung a quarter of ripening elk meat from a pole, then stationed Ed's pickup truck some distance off and sideways to the bait, with the windows rolled down. From here I could take a carefully rested shot out the window and be absolutely sure of the kill.

I put my loaded rifle in the truck cab, but it was too early to start my stakeout as it was still a while from evening light and early dusk.

Ed and I decided to go to the cook tent. He could bring his rifle there, so if the bear came early and we heard him we could dispatch him from the tent.

Now it happened that this was the evening of the Joe Louis versus Joe Walcott heavyweight title fight, and since I had been a boxer in the Army I was keen to hear the blow-by-blow report of the match on the radio.

We sat in the cook tent listening to the fight, not thinking much about the bear.

By the time the fight was over dusk was well upon us, and in fact I should already have been on the stand.

At any rate, as the match ended I stepped outside the tent to let my eyes grow accustomed to the poor light and there, not two feet away from me, stood a good-sized grizzly.

I thought it prudent not to make any quick movements so I said, quietly, "Ed, come out here."

Ed did just that, but he failed to bring his rifle.

Here we were in the dark close enough to this bear to rub its back and not even one firearm between us. I had that terrible feeling that you get when you find yourself in a very bad place and you know, absolutely, that you are there because you and nobody else have managed matters with disgusting incompetence.

Fortunately the bear decided there was too much company for his liking and slipped away into the night.

By the next morning I had mulled the issue over considerably and I questioned the crew.

The crew to a man swore they had been harassed by this bear to the point where they were afraid to go out of the tent.

Yet Ed and I had stood so close to the bear he could have taken both of us out with one swipe of a forepaw. Something did not add up here, but the crew insisted I track and destroy the bear. It was that or they would leave the camp.

So we set about tracking the bear up into the timber. About a quarter of a mile after we entered the timber we came on a patch of ground about twenty-five yards across that looked for all the world as though some one had dug it up in preparation for planting a garden.

Then we saw the half-buried remains of a partly eaten bear and we knew the story.

Two bears had met here and fought a terrible battle to the death. The victor had been eating for some while on his defeated foe.

We retreated quickly from that place because you do not threaten even the most benign-appearing bear by hanging around where he has cached the remains of a kill.

That discovery ended our bear hunt. We reckoned the winner had been our bear of last evening; the loser, the bear that had harassed the camp.

The camp experienced no further trouble ...

Black bears are not as large, powerful and fast as grizzlies, but in most respects they should be treated with similar caution.

I had been dealing with grizzlies a good deal when one day I was sent to take care of a black bear which had been raiding a work camp.

My son Hugh accompanied me, and when we arrived at the camp we set our tent and laid out our sleeping bags, then went to the cook trailer to visit the cook. I wanted to ask him about what the bear had been doing and particularly what times of the day the animal usually came around. A bear often keeps to quite a uniform daily schedule, and if he comes to your garbage can at five o'clock for a day or two, the chances are good that he will show up around the same time on the third and fourth days.

I had with me a Lee Enfield jungle carbine in .303 calibre. This was a handy rifle for the work at hand and it has a detachable magazine. I took my rifle with me to the cook trailer in order to clean it while I talked with the cook. On entering I removed the magazine, since it carried a full load of cartridges, and put it down on the table.

So far I was being sensible enough, but when I left the trailer to go back to our tent I made one of the sort of notorious oversights with which I occasionally get myself into big trouble. I brought my rifle with me but left the magazine full of cartridges sitting on the table. Perhaps I had been too much around grizzly bears lately and felt contemptuous toward black bears.

Along about five o'clock in the morning, a while after daybreak, I heard the bear in the supply tent, which was not far from our sleeping tent. I came out of the tent with my rifle in hand with the intention of dashing to the cook trailer for my magazine and cartridges.

The bear had a different plan and chased me back into the tent. Several times I tried to get to the trailer and each time the bear chased me back in the tent. Fortunately the bear did not follow me into the tent.

Finally we planned a somewhat improved strategy. On my next dash to the trailer, Hugh would set up a huge commotion of hollering and shouting as a diversion to distract the bear from such close attention to my movements.

The ploy worked, and this time I got to the trailer door. On my way I saw the cook was looking out the window watching the events and I thought good, he'll let me in as soon as I get to the door.

But he did not let me in, for fear, I suppose that he would not get the door closed in time to stop the bear coming in as well.

There was just enough space under the trailer for me to crawl into as the bear came charging again in my direction, and fortunately the bear did not crawl after me. He just stood guard, ready to deal with me whenever I might have the audacity to come out.

Then I began a discussion with the cook through the floor of the trailer.

"Why the hell didn't you let me in?"

"The bear was right behind you."

"Of course the bear was right behind me! That's why I had to get in. My damned cartridges are in there on the table."

"Yeah. I see 'em."

"Well, put them out the door so I can get hold of them!"

"No way. That bear's out there. I ain't openin' that door."

"Open the damned door just a crack and drop the cartridges out!"

"Wait a while. Maybe the bear will go away."

"Maybe the bear will come under this trailer after me! You drop those shells out the door or I will beat the hell out of you and feed you to the bears after I get out of this mess!"

Finally I got the cook as afraid of what I would do to him later as he was of opening the door just wide enough to drop the magazine-load of cartridges through. When it dropped on the ground my hand was ready and waiting to shoot out and snatch it into cover.

Never have I been so glad to hear the satisfying click of a magazine full of cartridges go home beneath the chamber of the rifle.

I went to the bolt and chambered a round. Then I sneaked out to the edge of cover again, steadied the sights just behind the bear's ears and squeezed off the round.

Then came the welcome blast and the nice recoil of the rifle into my shoulder and I could breathe again. I called Hugh out of the tent and told the cook he ought to get one behind the ear as well.

We struck our tent and left. The cook could get someone else to haul the bear away.

BEAR TRAP

Stephen Herrero

Dr. Stephen Herrero is the author of the best-selling book Bear Attacks: Their Causes and Avoidance, *and one of the foremost experts on bear behaviour in North America. But, as he admits in this story, even the most experienced biologists sometimes miscalculate when they are around grizzlies!*

ONE of two really close calls that I have had with a grizzly bear occurred as we were releasing a large male grizzly from a trap. In August 1977 an ignorant person left a horse carcass outside the fenced Cascade Sanitary Landfill in Banff National Park, and the dead horse attracted several grizzly bears. After the park wardens discovered the carcass, it was moved into the fenced landfill. A large, aggressive male grizzly bear bent two-inch steel fence posts and tore cyclone fencing to get at the carcass. This bear was trapped while inside the landfill.

On the morning of August 19, Andy Anderson, the chief warden, asked me if I would help in the relocation and also if I would photograph the bear after it was released. The wardens had decided not to drug the bear before releasing it, and so it would not be marked and photographs might be useful in identifying it ...

I knew that a grizzly coming out of a trap might try to attack people nearby. I vividly remember the grizzly's huge, black head banging against the bars of the trap as I approached. Between his eyes there was a raw spot from where he had hit his head on the trap. As I came near, he did it again while swatting the bars with his paws and making loud, blowing noises. The trap shook violently with his motions. My field notes state: "He looks like he could be trouble on the move ... "

Four of us, in two trucks, set off to relocate the bear in the backcountry. After a long, bouncing ride over a dirt road we set up for the release. The truck with the bear in the trap was in front with its engine running and we had a remote release for the trap door. Facing the other way, and one hundred feet distant in the second truck, was warden Jack Willman with a .308 rifle, biologist Luigi Morgantini, and myself. Both Luigi and I had cameras to get pictures of the bear as he left the trap.

Luigi had never seen a wild grizzly bear before, and so I warned him about the potential danger. I left our engine running as a further precaution. Luigi and I hung just outside the half-opened doors with our cameras. Jack sat in the middle seat with the rifle. I was on the driver's side.

We were ready, or so we thought. The guillotine gate of the bear trap was raised, and we waited. Nothing happened. Johnny Nyland, who was driving the other truck, jerked the trap back and forth. Still no response from the bear. Johnny threw his Stetson hat in a neat arc that ended with the hat sailing in front of the trap door. The bear didn't move.

We closed the trap door and decided to try to lure the bear out by building a "straw man" in the road in front of the bear. We propped a broom up with rocks, draped a canvas over it, and put a hat on our man. We repositioned trucks and people as before. Not really expecting anything dramatic, Johnny raised the trap door.

The huge, black grizzly bounded out and in a fraction of a second hit our straw man, biting the broomstick in half and sending canvas flying in ripped pieces. All this delayed the bear no more than a second or two and he continued galloping toward our truck. I glanced to my right and saw Luigi still hanging on his door taking pictures. I shouted at him to get inside. In the next instant, the bear hit the fender on my side with his paw and tried to climb onto the hood but slipped. For a long, frightening instant, I stared the grizzly in the eyes, fearing that he would come through the window. Luigi was inside and I hit the gas. The engine sputtered and then caught. The bear slid completely off the hood as we pulled away but ran alongside the door on my side for about a hundred feet. Then he dropped back, swerved off the road, and ran into the woods. We slowly regained our composure.

In organizing the release so as to get pictures of the bear for future identification, I had erred badly in getting our vehicle too close to the bear. At a full run I knew that it would take him only a few seconds to reach us, but I thought that we could be under way in that time. I had forgotten that Luigi was inexperienced with bears, and I expected things of him that I should not have.

BEAR ABOUT TOWN

Rick Kunelius

In 1980, sanitary landfills in the mountain parks were closed. Bear-proof garbage containers were installed in the townsites and campgrounds, and all garbage was trucked outside the parks for disposal. After more than ninety years, the era of garbage-habituated bears all but came to an end.

Black bear numbers declined following the big cleanup. In 1986, Parks Canada initiated a study to assess the population and status of black bears in Banff Park. As part of the study, a young bear named Kootenay was relocated to the Banff area from Radium, B.C. Kootenay had been habituated to human food in Radium and soon found his way into the town of Banff. Normally this would have been grounds for further relocation or elimination, but the Banff wardens decided the radio-collared bear could be used to monitor sloppy handling of garbage around the townsite. Kootenay became Banff's "Warden Bear." When he got into garbage, those responsible were reprimanded or fined. But most of the time, this placid, easy-going bear simply roamed the margins of the town, feeding on natural foods and watching the antics of its human inhabitants.

Park warden Rick Kunelius took a special interest in Kootenay and, for nearly seven years, worked diligently to ensure his survival. Most everyone in Banff got to know Kootenay during that period, but no one knew this amazing and lovable bear as well as Warden Rick.

MY most memorable day with Kootenay occurred one Sunday in June. At 09:00, a radio call came into the dispatch centre informing us that a black bear was lying about in the Cascade Gardens behind the Park Administration building. It had been there for a while and did not look like it was about to leave. The gardens are a major tourist attraction and by 11:00 the after-breakfast Sunday tourist crowd would be arriving in great numbers. It wouldn't do to have a bear around.

Well-watered and fertilized lawn grass is an attractive food for bears. I suppose it is similar to equisetum, or horsetail, a basic early-season staple for bears in our area. It is not often that one sees them grazing on a lawn of short grass when there are other succulent plants available.

Any excuse would do to get out of the office on a nice day. We grabbed the telemetry equipment, in case it might be a radio-collared bear, and headed across town. We dialed Kootenay's frequency and, sure enough, as we crossed the bridge toward the Administration building, the signal became clearer and clearer. Through the gates and around the back, we found him there, lying on the lawn, calmly munching grass. He chewed at everything he could reach from his prone position before he got up to wander over to another spot. There were numerous tourists about, enjoying the spectacle immensely. What an opportunity, I thought, to maximize the visitors' experience instead of chasing the bear away. The time to chase him would come soon enough when the crowds arrived and control of the situation could no longer be assured.

I had what some people considered an attitude problem. I've always believed the mandate of the National Parks is to maximize the visitors' enjoyment of the park and its wildlife. This means providing the opportunity to observe wildlife as long as they are not endangering themselves or harassing the animals.

We stayed in sight of Kootenay and talked to countless visitors, explaining that this black bear did not have an aggressive bone in his body. He had grown up in the National Park and had no reason to fear humans. Almost everyone was surprised to learn that bears are primarily vegetarians and that grass is a bigger part of their diet than meat. A few people, it seemed, were miffed that Kootenay was indifferent to them. Perhaps they had told stories to their kids of how they had once scared away a dangerous bear, and this bear did not fit the image. But everyone shared in the fascination.

Inevitably, as noon approached, there were more and more kids running about and people trying to get closer for pictures. Confusion began to reign. It was time to get Kootenay out of there. So I put on my Stetson hat, to look a bit more official, and walked over to him, hoping he would head out along the back trail and into the woods.

"Come on, Kootenay, time to go. Just head on up the trail and out the back way. It's getting too crowded. You've had your fun, now get out of town for a while."

He may not have understood the words, but he seemed to grasp the intent, for he ambled off toward the woods.

He soon reached the fence separating the flower gardens from the adjacent woods and a tall turnstile that allows people through but keeps elk and deer out. Kootenay could have fit through on all fours, or he could have gone through on his back legs while keeping balance with his front paws on the turnstile, or he could have simply climbed the fence post and popped over. Instead he chose to climb the turnstile itself. When he reached the top, he stood up and balanced as if to wave "so long," then scampered down the other side and ran off into the woods.

Once again, he got me. I returned to the office and, over coffee, told everyone how the little bugger climbed over the turnstile and turned to wave goodbye. No one was overly surprised; they had all heard too many Kootenay anecdotes.

It wasn't long before another call came into the dispatch centre. There was a bear reported behind the Whyte Museum, smack in the centre of town. The back of the museum has a large yard running down to Bow Avenue and the river. There is always a lot of tourist traffic along Bow Avenue, and Central Park is nearby, full of picnic tables. Not a good place for a bear on a Sunday afternoon.

I was dreading that it might be Kootenay, displaying behaviour much bolder than he ever had before. We did not waste any time getting to the scene. I expected a huge crowd of bear-watchers, but there was nothing out of the ordinary. We drove through the traffic searching for a "bear jam," but it was just a normal summer Sunday. The signal from Kootenay's radio collar indicated he was somewhere across the river, west of the Administration building. He had a day bed in that area, where I often found him, so I was confident he was not the source of our report. There are trees and bushes in the back yard of the museum where a bear could hide, so we kept looking. As we drove around the block, my partner shouted "There he is!" Then, as I tried to find a spot to pull over in the heavy traffic, I heard my partner mutter dejectedly, "Forget it."

Across the yard, between a shrub and the building, was a lifesize silhouette of a black bear. The one-dimensional cut-out could only be seen from a certain angle, and if you did not stop to look closely, then it certainly looked like a real bear. Who knows how long it had been there. One thing was certain, it was too much fun to take down. But I imagine that silhouette startled more than a few people as they took a shortcut through the backyard after dark that summer.

Confident that Kootenay was napping in his day bed above Cave Avenue, I returned to the office. About 2:30 my wife called me at the office with an update on Kootenay. Just after I had cruised past the museum and Central Park to discover the silhouette bear, Eleanor arrived in the park to join her aerobics class, which was meeting there to perform for charity. About halfway through their routines, one of the girls screamed "BEAR!" They all froze. Directly across the river, standing among the spruce trees near the shore, and peering directly at the ladies, was indeed a bear.

Not just any bear. It was a big, dark, glossy bear, and it kept staring at them. Some of the ladies thought "maybe it's a grizzly, we gotta get outa here." Then Eleanor got a better look at the bear.

"Relax ladies, it's just Kootenay. He doesn't have a mean bone in his body. He just likes to watch."

Most of the participants knew who Kootenay was and fear soon turned to curiosity. The class resumed their exercises and Kootenay continued to stand across the river and watch. About the same time as the class ended, he became bored and moved on upstream into the woods and out of sight.

It was a busy, event-filled weekend in Banff. There was also a relay race, and the finish line was over by the Recreation Centre on the north side of town. I did not want to get involved doing traffic control for the runners, so I kept a low profile in the office. Toward the end of the afternoon, I thought I would take the telemetry equipment and check on Kootenay one last time on the way home. Might as well go via the race and see how things were going there as well.

I heard a faint beep on Kootenay's frequency as I left the office, but soon lost it as I drove eastward. Heading back west again the signal strength improved as I approached the west entrance to town. I stopped by the Timberline Hotel, where I received a signal bearing indicating that he was somewhere in the area of the Fenland bog. I moved over a kilometre to take a second bearing and the two signals intersected at the relay-race finish line near the Recreation Centre.

Not wanting to alarm anyone, I casually drove down the road toward the race finish with my ears tuned to that little beeping signal coming from Kootenay's collar. It is not easy to drive a truck, switch back and forth between directional antennas, and look nonchalant all at the same time. As I drew even with the finish line the signal strength peaked off to the right, while the runners peeled off to the left. Our bear was over there by the Forty Mile Creek picnic area, watching. He could hear, smell, and see what was going on, but over one hundred people had no idea he was even there.

When I got home I filled in Eleanor on the day's events. She was as fascinated with this bear as I was and never tired of hearing about his latest adventures. Neither of us could let it go, so after dinner we headed out for one more location check. This one took us a little while because the signal was being blocked by buildings and bouncing around all over. "Let's go back to the last seen point," I said. From the Norquay overpass the signal was clear and sharp, and the antenna pointed straight toward the Tunnel Mountain campground.

I was wishing I was in uniform with an official truck and a radio, for if he was in the campground scrounging for human food, we had to get him out of there quick. As we crested the hill toward the campground, the signal became clean and sharp, but as we came closer to the campground it began to fade. So he wasn't in the campground after all. Perhaps he was by the old water tower, another favourite day-bed area. From the water tower, the signal pointed back to the motels and the hostel. Somewhat perplexed and wondering what could be attracting him, we drove to the west edge of the campground. He had to be close, so we parked and started out on foot toward the best signal. It wasn't five minutes before we were startled by a rustle in the bush ahead of us. Kootenay bolted off into the forest; all we saw was a flash of dark brown fur. We were almost on top of him when he took off, so we moved to where he had been. The long grass was still flattened and it was clear where he had been sitting—under the trees, behind a bush, watching the kids at the hostel playing volleyball.

He loved to watch.

VIII
RENEWING THE SPIRIT

The animal that impresses me most, the one I find myself liking more and more, is the grizzly ... His is a dignity and power matched by no other in the North American wilderness. To share a mountain with him for a while is a privilege and an adventure like no other.

— Andy Russell, *Grizzly Country* —

IN THE SOCIETY OF GRIZZLIES

Andy Russell

In producing his book and a film on grizzly bears, Andy Russell followed the track of the great bear into the last pockets of wilderness throughout North America. But one of his most intimate glimpses into grizzly bear society occurred near the end of his project in 1964, literally in his own backyard in the southern Alberta foothills.

ERHAPS the most startling instance of the acceptance of one species by another that I have encountered in grizzly country occurred here on our ranch in the spring of 1964, when we were more or less adopted by five grizzlies. One of these was a somewhat reluctant and suspicious old male whose amorous interests in a female put him in the role of a participant with certain reservations, but the others were remarkably trusting and unconcerned.

At the beginning severe weather conditions undoubtedly had a bearing on their strange behavior. A rather open, warm winter had culminated in heavy falls of snow, and the mountains west of the ranch were buried deep in the loose stuff. Conditions were not enhanced by a very late spring break-up, and when the grizzlies emerged from den in early May, they found their usual ranges uninhabitable. So they moved to lower ground.

One overcast evening in early June, Kay and I were in our cottage, while twelve-year-old daughter Anne was busy with some project at the lodge a hundred yards away up the hill. Son Gordon was busy in the shop back of the cottage, and the lights were on in all the buildings. Gordon heard a noise in the yard, and looking out through the open door of the shop, he was startled to see four grizzlies standing on the road not twenty yards away. A medium-sized female and two large cubs were standing in front of a huge old boar, and all the bears were obviously intrigued with their surroundings. There was much snorting, sniffing, and excited popping of jaws as the bears alternately reared up to inspect the place. Finally the female and cubs walked right past the cottage door, following the driveway about twenty feet away. The boar was alarmed and doubled back into the aspens and saskatoon brush out of sight. Meanwhile the sow and cubs continued on through the yard and disappeared into the brush down the hill. When we went up to the lodge in the misty dusk a few minutes later, we could still hear them whoofing and sniffing in the thick growth below the buildings.

Then all was quiet for an hour or more. Anne went out to get something she had left at the cottage, while we were reading around the big fireplace. None of us gave it any thought until she burst through the door and breathlessly exclaimed about meeting a grizzly on the path between the houses. The porch light was on, and we went to investigate; the sow grizzly was standing inside its ring of light in a little hollow below the veranda, huffing and snapping her jaws. Somehow she had become separated from the cubs, which we heard in the brush behind the lodge having some kind of animated argument. The light streaming through the front windows was broken into shafts by the mist, making an eerie setting for the sound of big animals moving around the perimeter of the yard. The sounds continued for some time, and then the family apparently got together again, for things quieted down for the rest of the night.

Naturally we supposed that the grizzlies had blundered unintentionally into the yard and that they would leave for good. But next morning when I stepped out under a bright sky for a look through the binoculars, the female and cubs were sprawled in the sun in a little meadow surrounded by aspens about five hundred yards down the slope, just across the fence line separating our place from that of a neighbor. They had found the carcass of a heifer that had died about six weeks earlier, and they had fed on it. Later that day we saw two more grizzlies, the same big male of the previous evening and a smaller bear, another male about four years old. All were staying in the general vicinity of the carcass, but the two males were shy. The sow, however, seemed to have decided that everything was made to order for their well-being, for she and the cubs continued to be very much at home.

We were somewhat concerned, regardless of their peaceful intentions, for this is ranching country, and while it is populated by very reasonable, friendly people, we knew these grizzlies would likely precipitate some powder-burning if they proceeded to walk into ranch yards and stand about discussing the layout in bear language. If possible, we wanted to prevent them from getting into trouble before the snow melted enough to allow them back into their normal range up in the mountains. That evening Charlie and John took a horse we did not want to keep back up onto a butte west of the buildings, well inside our property, and shot it. The grizzlies must have been keeping tabs on the whole procedure, for they immediately accepted this handout. By daylight next morning we found that they had fed heavily on it.

Thus began a three-week period of the most interesting experience with grizzlies we have ever had here on the ranch. At the beginning of this session the sow was evidently mating with the larger male. We could only guess, the cover being so heavy over most of the country that keeping tabs on the romance of grizzlies would be like repeatedly finding the proverbial needle in the haystack. She often left the two cubs alone at the horse carcass, where we saw them regularly and photographed them several times at close range. Later, when the mating was over, one cub went back to her, but the other somehow got separated, staying by himself up on Cottonwood Creek a couple of miles to the west. And we grew accustomed to seeing grizzly tracks near our home, but not once did the bears show any inclination to get into mischief.

Strangely enough they did not at first show any desire to make an appearance anywhere else, although there were two occupied ranches within a mile. But then the sow found a dead cow on an adjoining property along the Cottonwood, and she and the cub and the smaller male took turns feeding on it. These activities were confined primarily to the night hours, but as time went on they became bolder. When choosing to feed in the daylight, the grizzlies could be seen from the highway beyond, and we knew it would be only a matter of time before someone took a shot at them (spring bear season was open at that time), so I decided to give them a scare.

One afternoon when Kay spotted the female going toward this carcass, I took a rifle and followed. Coming down the steep, wooded bank of the creek, I approached within fifty yards of her and the cub without their giving me more than a brief glance. The cub was a bit edgy about my presence but did not run. I fired a shot into the ground under the sow's head. The cub jumped nervously at the impact of the bullet, but the sow just swiveled on her feet and stared at me long and hard, as though to say, "What the hell did you do a thing like that for?" For answer I put another shot into the ground beside her. The cub started away, but when the mother surprisingly chose to ignore me and returned to her feeding, it came back. I then walked down toward the grizzlies and yelled. Both bears then moved toward the creek, and as they began to cross it, I put a third shot into the water close to them. I was using a powerful .358 Winchester, and its heavy bullet made a considerable racket on hitting the water; but even this did not hurry the old bear very much. Perhaps she knew I had no intention of hurting her. The more I have to do with grizzlies, the more I am impressed with their seeming ability to study and come to know what a man is thinking. Certainly she left reluctantly, although she showed no anger or desire to fight about it.

A little later I found the young male feeding on the carcass alone. Although again armed with the rifle, I decided to try something different on him. Keeping out of sight and circling down the creek to keep the wind in my favor, I came up very quietly from behind a fold of ground to within about fifteen yards of him. The grizzly was lying on his belly with his hindquarters toward me, completely occupied with his feeding. Reaching into the rib cage of the dead cow with a front paw, he would claw out a juicy tidbit, hold it up, and lick it off his claws. If feeding on such fare could be termed delicate, he was feeding with certain delicacy, although the air was so thick with the smell of rotten flesh, it almost lifted my hat off.

After watching the grizzly for a minute or two, I suddenly bellowed, "Get out of here and stay out!"

Never have I seen a more surprised animal. He came back on his heels like a released spring, half rearing and swiveling toward me, and then he leaped away like a shot out of a gun. He covered about forty feet or more in three bounds, hit the creek throwing water high in the air, and fairly flew up the slope beyond. He took the hint, for he did not come back. My only regret was that no part of this bit of action was successfully recorded on film.

The she-grizzly and the cub continued visiting the carcass as though nothing had happened until it was almost completely eaten up. She became increasingly careless and walked up to a neighbor's door one night and inspected the box of a parked pickup truck. The neighbor was aroused by the ranch dog and fired a shot at her in the dark. It wounded her only superficially, but it taught her a lesson and marked the end of her visit in the locality.

The grapevine of the wilds seemed to pass the word around very quickly, for almost overnight all the grizzlies except the cub up at the head of the Cottonwood left for the sanctuary of the Park and did not return.

The lone cub came down close to our buildings as the season progressed, and often it came close to our door. This was a pretty, golden-brown young animal weighing about two hundred pounds. Although the sex of individual bears is always hard to determine, we decided it was a male and christened him Storm, after a bear character I had written about in a magazine story sometime previously.

Storm was a very mannerly, self-effacing grizzly with a built-in shyness, great curiosity, and amazing willingness to join the life of our ranch without undue disturbance. He was very much intrigued by our house cat and bored with Anne's noisy terrier, Blackie. His curiosity almost drove the cat into a nervous breakdown, but his restraint in taking no action against much belligerent barking and rushing on the part of the dog built that small canine's ego up to almost unbearable proportions.

One morning very early Kay and I were wakened by sounds like nothing on earth. Upon investigation we found the cat in the throes of feline hysterics on the top step of the back door. Storm was standing in the open end of the breezeway with his head cocked to one side, fascinated by the cat's vocal display but showing no inclination to investigate any further. When Kay firmly but politely told him to leave, he loped away into the brush. Meanwhile the cat shot into the house to stand in the middle of the living-room floor, the picture of outrage, her back in a bow and her tail like a bent stovepipe.

This was only one of a number of visits by Storm that were effusively greeted by Blackie, whose rushing around and shrill barking was almost ignored. Although the dog's size did not much surpass the cat's, this caused him to show not the slightest fear of the bear. What amazed us was the grizzly's tolerance of the little terrier.

When Kay began putting up preserves late in the summer, she spent a good deal of time picking the lush, tasty saskatoon berries. On these expeditions she was invariably accompanied by the dog and quite often joined the grizzly in the same berrypatch. The dog spent its time rushing back and forth with great fanfare and importance between her and the grizzly, while the young bear and Kay proceeded to pick berries, each knowing exactly where the other was located. While a bit noisy, the arrangement eliminated any chance of an embarrassing head-on encounter in the thick jungle of summer foliage, and things worked out satisfactorily for all concerned.

We had not adopted a grizzly. A grizzly had adopted us. Storm was indeed very gentle but still a wild bear. Never, as far as we know, did our acquaintance show himself in a neighbor's yard. Even when he came into ours, he came with a certain shyness, and not once did his curiosity cause him to leave so much as a claw mark on any of our possessions. Since his visits were loudly announced by Blackie, there were no surprises at close range, a circumstance he likely appreciated as much as we did. Not once did he growl or show any irritation at frequent invasions into his berrypatches. We were an honored and accepted part of his society. It was a rare and revealing look at one of the many sides of grizzly character …

At first snow last fall Storm left us to head up into the mountains, and we have never seen him since. As I write this, he is likely curled up in a warm den dreaming of warm summer days and luscious berries. Maybe he will come back when the glacier lilies bloom again.

Storm proved that at least one grizzly could tolerate humans. Not only were we made aware of the relationship possible between man and grizzly, but another thread was revealed in the fascinating pattern of nature's tapestry of the wilds.

TRACKS IN THE TONQUIN

Sid Marty

Sid Marty worked as a park warden in Yoho, Jasper, and Banff National Parks during the late 1960s and early 1970s. One of his best assignments was in Jasper's Tonquin Valley where he spent a summer in one of the Rockies' most scenically situated backcountry warden cabins with his wife, Myrna. In late September, Sid bade farewell to the valley by making one last patrol, following the trail of a sow grizzly and her three cubs.

DOWN below the cabin, the lake water was tinted black in contrast to the white clarity of its banks, and a belt of cloud girdled the Ramparts, ermine against their royal purple. It was a great day for climbers wanting to plan new routes. The light snow had etched out every rough line in the towering walls that had appeared smooth yesterday. Now, every ledge and bulge that would hold snow or a climber's foot was sketched out in bold relief. I took the water pails down where the creek smoked in the chill air and stopped in mid-stride at the sight of a message printed for me in the snow.

There were tracks all around the cabin and tracks around the tree that held our meat cache, a wooden, screened box lashed high off the ground. The tracks looked as if a big man and three kids had walked barefoot around the cabin while we slept. There was a wide sole mark, and five toe indentations in each print, just like a human foot. But at the tip of each toe was a round hole poked through the snow and into the soft earth beneath it, made by the four-inch-long claws of a grizzly sow. The tracks of three cubs followed hers around the cabin.

"Prrr-ock," went the raven from its perch and was answered by its cohort in a stand of trees to the north that separated the cabin from another wide meadow. I looked to where the bird pointed like an animated weather-cock, and saw between the trees four black shapes already a mile away, the big sow moving steadily toward the forest edge, the three cubs rambling after.

The snow had made her restless. She had stayed down near the head of the Astoria for as long as the range would permit, feeding on the carcass of a moose she'd killed. The ravens led me to the carcass, half-buried under dead limbs and moss the sow had raked over it; the bone marrow, an unhealthy grey, showed it to be an old or a sick animal. Easy prey. Now she would change her range for a while, maybe head down Meadow Creek to get below the snow belt, and feed on what was left of the berry crop at that lower altitude. She needed plenty of high calorie food, because from now on the need to lay on fat would dominate her existence until the real winter set in, driving her and the cubs into their winter den. Her appetite was stimulated by the five-month-long famine that would soon be upon her, and nothing would distract her from trying to satisfy her belly, not even the demands of motherhood ...

Fortunately, there were no campers left in the Tonquin Valley. The rain that had preceded the snow had sent them packing down to the highway. But there was always the chance that more people would be hiking in via Portal Creek and Maccarib Pass, coming in to the Tonquin where Maccarib Creek flows in at the north end of the lake. The bear was headed that way so I decided to follow her and learn what I could about her routes and her temperament. If I met any hikers on the way, there'd be good opportunity to prevent run-ins with the bears by making sure they kept a clean camp, with their grub tied up in a tree.

The horses were out of sight. "Ho, boys!" I called and heard the "pong" of Toby's old brass bell float to me across the meadows, but the sound echoed from the mountains on both sides of the valley, and you could never fix his direction from the first note. "Oats, Toby!" I yelled, like every morning, and heard the bell go "pong, pong," as he lifted his head and nodded a yes to his belly at the prospect of grain. The horses had drifted up the lake shore toward Tom's camp. I thought tonight I'd feed them in the corral, in case they tried to pull out on me, and head down Meadow Creek for Dominion Prairie. That was down on the

Yellowhead Highway, safe from early snow. Even with hobbles, they'd pull out if they sensed a blizzard coming, jumping like kangaroos with the front feet moving together, a trick any mountain horse knows well.

I went out with a halter to where they had turned to watch for me, the snow still clinging in patches on their rumps, steam rising from their wet backs. I slipped the hobbles and haltered my saddle horse and the others followed, walking stiffly at first, taking small, shuffling steps as if the hobbles were still on their front feet. We went up to the cabin.

Myrna had seen the tracks. "I'm going to follow her for a while," I told her. "I want to see where she goes, figure out her range a bit better."

"I guess you'll have to bushwhack," she said.

"Probably. I doubt she'll stay on the trails. I may have to lead the horse and climb if she goes up high."

"It's all right. I wouldn't mind taking it easy today. Really," she added, seeing my contentious look.

I'd been expecting more of an argument; she fooled me, as usual.

After breakfast, I buckled on my leather chaps, then went out and tightened Toby's cinch. Myrna brought our coffee out on the porch and we drank it in the sunlight, savouring the flavour of the brew and the smell of spruce and wet meadow grass. I watched the horse pawing impatiently at the snow, anxious to be moving in the chill air. I finished my coffee and set my cup down.

"Hold the fort, sugar," I told her and went over to the horse and untied his lines, "it may be dark before I get back."

"Write if you find work," she said, watching me swing on. "Shouldn't you take the rifle?"

"Naw. The trouble with that rifle is that once you have it, you have a tendency to think you're safe. Bears don't like the smell of gun grease. Best not to get close enough for them to smell it in the first place."

"Good advice," she said. "Just see that you follow it."

I grinned and rode out on the track of the bears. The snow made it easy work, but it would be melted by mid-afternoon, so I took a short-cut across the meadow at the trot, aiming to pick up her sign on the far side again. Just before the tracks led into the woods, Toby shied at a dark object half hidden in the willow shrubs. It was a dark green pile of bear crap, splashed with the brilliant red of soapberry. I got off to have a look at it because a bear's droppings will often give insights into a bear's state of health that would be dangerous to try to obtain by means of a more intimate inspection of the animal. The crap on hand was still conveniently firmed up by the night's cold, despite the enematic effect of the soapberries on the bear's digestive tract. What they see in those acridly bitter lumps of poison is beyond me, but they will spend days gorging themselves at berry time, using their claws as rakes to gather in the berries, or simply eat them branches and all. The size of the scats identified them as the sow's and not the cubs', and the green colour meant she'd been feeding almost completely on vegetable matter, not flesh, which gives a characteristically dark blackish colour to the stool. With a stick I broke it up, looking for bone fragments and animal hair and checking for parasites, but found nothing but vegetable fibre. The sow was healthy, which was good, since it made her less likely to try and steal human food out of desperation.

A big rock fell and clattered down the wall of Paragon Peak on the far side of the lake. It rolled down the talus slope and into the lake with a splash. The sun was fully up, and the good tracking would not last long. Tom Vinson's chainsaw rattled a half mile to the left, as he cut deadfall on the wood permit I'd issued to him. He would buck it into eight-foot logs to be skidded to his camp when the snow was deep enough for them to slide easily.

The bear tracks led into the dark woods, and I reined in for a moment to let my eyes adjust to the dim light, after the dazzle of snow in the bright meadow. The tracks meandered indecisively on the trail of a marten, backing up in disgust from the marten's pissing post where the pungent weasel scent had assaulted the sow's nose. We came out into a narrow meadow at the foot of an avalanche slope. Here the trail, which had been steadily gaining altitude, as if to bypass the campground, detoured abruptly down a creek to the first tent site, where much scuffling and arguing had gone on over some fish guts that somebody had heaved into the creek, and where one cub had been roundly cuffed out of the way and sent rolling down the slope like a ball to learn some manners. There were a few bright scales clinging to the rocks; other than that, the camp's water supply, fouled by man, had been purified again by the bears, our resident sanitary inspectors.

The sow knew all about campgrounds. She had taken the cubs on a tour all around the tent sites, and their tracks were in the snow on top of the camp tables. I had cleaned up that campground just a few days ago, burning the paper and bagging cans and bottles to be packed out on the horses. The place was spotless, free of human pollution, or at least that's how it appeared to me. The critical nose of the bear mocked my efforts. All through the campground there were little pockets of snow and earth dug up and in each one was a garbage souvenir that campers had buried under a pile of leaves, covered with a rock or stuffed down a ground-squirrel burrow. The sow had scented each one out and dug it up for me; an orange peel, a chocolate bar wrapper, chewed into a wad and spat out again, tin cans, plastic bags, beer bottle caps, and Kleenex—soggy, pink, and ubiquitous—all scattered obscenely on the immaculate white of the snow. I slumped in the saddle and sighed when I came to the old garbage pit that one erstwhile group had dug with their trusty war surplus trenching tools. They had filled the pit in behind them with a couple of feet of dirt, probably figuring that the garbage had been neatly disposed of for all time. Two feet of loose dirt is not even a fair test to a bear's nose. Contemptuously she had raked it all out, spreading broken glass, tinfoil and plastic bags from hell to breakfast for me to clean up.

I tied the horse up and worked for an hour gathering up the smaller bits and pieces that would fit in Toby's saddlebags. The rest I stuffed into a burlap sack carried for that purpose, which I cached in the fork of a tree to be packed out later. Patches of grass were showing through the snow by the time the job was done, and the tracks were erased from the meadow beyond the camp. Back in the saddle, I circled the camp until we cut her sign, picking it up on a higher contour where the snow was shadowed from the melting warmth of the sun under a canopy of spruce. She'd gone up the mountain in a straight line, headed for timberline and the higher meadows that lay beyond. The trail was an overgrown tunnel through the forest, the moss deeply indented by the feet of her ancestors, made impassable to us by the overhanging limbs and deadfall. A big spruce at the entrance was blazed and gouged by the claws of bears that had come this way over the years. A tuft of black hair was stuck to the trunk, glued in a stream of pitch that had flowed out of the wounded tree; memento of some old humpback that had paused to rub its back against the rough bark, relieving a colossal itch.

Toby stopped, his nostrils twitching, smelling bear. "Gitup," I told him, and we went switchbacking up the mountainside, working our way through the trees as we climbed back and forth across her trail, snapping off dead limbs and being generally about as quiet as a bull moose in rut as the horse lunged through the shintangle. The end of a snag slipped under the stirrup leather and Toby stopped, breathing hard. I got off and pulled it out, then began climbing up on foot, leading him. The sweat was running down my face by the time we made it out to timberline, walking through a stand of larch trees, their black branches wrapped with the spun gold of their changed needles. We contoured across to the north until I picked up her trail coming out of the timber near the edge of an old rockslide. She was hunting ground-squirrels and the hunting had been good. We came to a fresh dig where she had shifted a boulder weighing a quarter of a ton to get at the burrows beneath it. There were blood stains and a wisp of gold fur on the dirty snow, all that was left of the ground-squirrel colony.

The horse snorted and backed up nervously. Even I could smell the musky taint of grizzly bear in the ravished earth. An afternoon sun was warming the slopes, and the wind had changed in favour of the sow; blowing up my neck and carrying our scent towards her. A pika, a diminutive relative of the rabbit, squeaked and chittered with alarm from its vantage point halfway up a rockslide. Sensing the bear was near, I quickly got back on the horse and spurred him forward below the slide to where I could see a good line of escape leading down toward the valley of Maccarib Creek. Toby was skittish, worried now that he could no longer get wind of the bear, and not knowing in what direction to look.

She was watching us, but from where? I was sure that she wasn't below us in the timber; she would feel safer if she kept above us. There was nothing in sight on the steepening arc of the horizon; the green line of the meadow was marked only by scattered patches of dwarf spruce and the sharp ridges of Mount Clitheroe rising beyond it. I reined the horse in and waited; no sense moving until we figured out where she was. A flight of pink snow birds spiralled up from the forest below and flitted in a rose-coloured cloud across the patchy snow to land, noisily quarrelling on a clump of dwarf spruce two hundred feet above us. The sow stood up then with a roar and the small birds scattered and tumbled like pink fluff from her shoulders with high pitched, frightened cries.

Toby's ears went up like rockets and he took one step back and froze with his front legs braced. My feet tightened involuntarily in the stirrups, as I began to ease his head to the left again, wanting him pointed the right way, in case he ran into the timber, bucking. Standing seven feet high with her yellowed claws held out in front of her, the sow dominated the horizon, her black form etched against the snow and the blue of the sky, her silver-tipped ruff fanned out in the light. She weaved her head gently back and forth and sniffed sharply, reading our scent, and the sound shivered the air like a bone whistle or the note the wind will make on the lip of a chimney. I shook the reins lightly and Toby took a step sideways, wanting to keep his head toward her, watching. The cubs walked out of the bush then and stood up beside her. One of them dropped to all fours and walked a little ways down the hill towards us, curious to find out what we were.

Her hair was up. "Easy Toby," I said and kicked him around, urging him forward. She noticed the cub, dropped to all fours and came down the hill without warning, letting out a bellow when she ran over the cub in her haste, continuing on in a line that would take her to the right of us. The speed of her charge precluded any motion from us until she had already pulled up and turned to go back to the squalling cub. She cuffed him once, driving him uphill, and he shut up fast, scurrying after his siblings. Then they were gone over the crest and I knew the charge had been a bluff, made out of fear for the cub.

There had been no time to feel fear but now that she was gone I saw my hands trembling on the reins and felt the slightly nauseated churning in the gut that follows a surge of adrenalin and an accelerated heartbeat.

"Close enough, Toby," I told the horse and he stepped quickly down the slope following the tree line by way of an answer, snorting and shaking his head as if to say, "I told you so." In a few minutes we reached the mouth of a steep-walled ravine. Looking up, I saw the bears a quarter mile above us, moving quickly across the top of the meadow at the base of the cliffs. But she would have to go lower for a while to feed before taking them up to dig a winter den high on an avalanche slope. How long she stayed out after that would depend on her fat and the weather.

We rode down through the meadows, wary and alert, feeling the tension in the air that the presence of a grizzly creates, a tension that hones the senses to a sharp edge, so that they quicken to the slightest movement, the faintest noise or scent.

"Know how to tell a grizzly bear from a black bear?" an old timer asked me, many years ago. "Just climb a tree. Black bear will climb up after you. Old silvertip, he can't climb; so he'll just shake you out of the tree like a plum, if he don't tear it out by the roots."

In his hyperbole there is a serious message. Allowing the bears to roam at will admits a risk to existence that is at odds with the carefully controlled environments of men outside bear country. Here, the bears make the rules, and though the black bear is usually timid, and a tree is usually a safe refuge from the grizzly, you can't ever count on being completely free from danger.

Wilderness provides us with insights into our own animate nature, that we can experience nowhere else. Without the grizzly bear, the last great predator of lower North America, there is no wilderness, only tame, empty playgrounds that mock the pretensions of the adventurers who wander through them. While the bears survive, those of us who love wildness still have a refuge to retreat to from the sea of madness that surrounds it and cuts its corrosive channels more deeply, year by year.

PERMISSIONS

"The Bear Lodge" by John C. Ewers, from *The Blackfeet: Raiders on the North-western Plains* (Norman, OK: University of Oklahoma Press, 1958). © 1958 by the University of Oklahoma Press. Reprinted by permission of John C. Ewers and the University of Oklahoma Press.

"Legend of the Bear Spear" by Onesta (Blackfoot) as recorded by Walter McClintock, from *Old Indian Trails* (New York: Houghton Mifflin, 1923).

"The Nurturing Bear" is a Flathead tale paraphrased by David Rockwell, from *Giving Voice to Bear: North American Indian Myths, Rituals, and Images of the Bear* (Niwot, CO: Roberts Rinehart Publishers, 1991). Reprinted by permission of the University of Montana.

"A Stoney Bear Story" by Walter Wilcox, from *The Rockies of Canada* (New York: The Knickerbocker Press, 1900). Reproduced by permission of the Canadian Museum of Civilization.

"Hector Crawler and the Bear" by George McLean (Stoney) as recorded by Marius Barbeau, from *Indian Days on the Western Prairies* (Ottawa: Queen's Printer, 1965).

"'Things are Changing'" by Ella E. Clark from a story by William Gingrass (Kootenay), from *Indian Legends from the Northern Rockies* (Norman, OK: University of Oklahoma Press, 1966). © 1966 by the University of Oklahoma Press. Reprinted by permission of Ella E. Clark and the University of Oklahoma Press.

"The First Bear Story" by David Thompson, from *David Thompson's Narrative 1784–1812*, Richard Glover, ed. (Toronto: The Champlain Society, 1962).

"Grizzly Attacks on the Fraser River" by Simon Fraser, from *Simon Fraser: Letters & Journals, 1806–1808*, W. Kaye Lamb, ed. (Toronto: Macmillan of Canada, 1960). Reproduced by permission of W. Kaye Lamb.

"The Botanist and the Bear" by Thomas Drummond, in "Sketch of a Journey to the Rocky Mountains and to the Columbia River in North America," from *Botanical Miscellany*, Sir William J. Hooker, ed. (London: John Murray, 1830).

"Mr. O'B. and the Three Bears" by Viscount Milton and W.B. Cheadle, from *The North-West Passage by Land* (London: Cassell, Petter, and Galpin, 1865).

"Memories of a Bear Hunter" by Henry J. Moberly, from *When Fur was King* (Toronto: J.M. Dent & Sons, 1929).

"Adventures on the CPR Survey" by Robert M. Rylatt, from *Surveying the Canadian Pacific* (Salt Lake City: University of Utah Press, 1991).

"Grizzly in the Snow" by Col. P. Robertson-Ross, in "Robertson-Ross' Diary: Fort Edmonton to Wildhorse, B.C., 1972," Hugh A. Dempsey, ed., from *Alberta History*, Vol.9, No.3, 1961. Reprinted by permission of Hugh A. Dempsey.

"Tracks on the Trail" by Hugh E.M. Stutfield and J. Norman Collie, from *Climbs and Exploration in the Canadian Rockies* (London: Longmans, Green and Co., 1903).

"My Grizzly-bear Day" by William T. Hornaday, from *Camp-Fires in the Canadian Rockies* (New York: Charles Scribner's Sons, 1907).

"Testing a Theory" by R.M. Patterson, from *The Buffalo Head* (New York: William Sloan, 1961). Reprinted by permission of Mrs. R.M. Patterson.

"The Agony of Warden McDonald" by Sid Marty, from *Men from the Mountains* (Toronto: McClelland & Stewart, 1978). Used by permission, McClelland & Stewart, Inc. *The Canadian Publishers*.

"Stoppin' for a Smoke" by Frank Goble, from *The Trapper—Volume 2* (Cardston: Frank Goble, 1996). Reprinted by permission of Frank Goble.

"A Nocturnal Visit" by C.E. Millar, from the Charles Millar papers (Banff: Whyte Museum of the Canadian Rockies). Reprinted courtesy of the Chuck Millar Family.

"Shenanigans in Banff" by Pat Brewster, from *Wild Cards* (Banff: Estate of F.O. Brewster, 1982). Reprinted courtesy of the family of Dorothy Cranstone.

"Bruno the Bear" from *Scarlet and Gold*, 36th edition, 1954. Reprinted courtesy of the RCMP Veterans Association, Vancouver Division.

"Bear Bitten" from official correspondence, Jasper National Park, 1923. Jasper-Yellowhead Museum and Archives. Reprinted courtesy of the Jasper-Yellowhead Museum and Archives.

"Mouth-to-Mouth" by C.E. Millar, from the Charles Millar papers (Banff: Whyte Museum of the Canadian Rockies). Reprinted courtesy of the Chuck Millar Family.

"Edward's Grizzly Bear" by Ken Jones as told to Lorne and Kim Tetarenko, from *Ken Jones—Mountain Man* (Calgary: Rocky Mountain Books, 1996). Reprinted by permission of Rocky Mountain Books.

"Bears in Jasper" by Nora Findlay, from *Jasper—A Backward Glance* (Jasper: Parks and People, 1992). Reprinted by permission of the publisher.

"The Nuisance Grounds" by Hugh M. Halliday, from *Wildlife Trails Across Canada* (Toronto: Thomas Allen, 1956).

"Bears, All the Time Bears" by Rudy Wiebe, from *Alberta—A Celebration* (Edmonton: Hurtig Publishers, 1979). Reprinted by permission of the author, 1998.

"The Man-eating Bears of Yarrow Creek" by Andy Russell, from *Grizzly Country* (New York: Alfred A. Knopf, 1967). Reprinted by permission of the publisher.

"Speaking of Bears" by Lawrence Burpee, from *On the Old Athabaska Trail* (London: Hurst & Blackett, 1927).

"It's Good to Be Alive" by N. Vernon-Wood, from *National Sportsman*, September 1936.

"The Jumping Bear" by Walter Nixon as told to Bruno Engler, from *A Mountain Life* (Canmore: Alpine Club of Canada, 1996). Reprinted courtesy of the Alpine Club of Canada.

"The Student Bear" by Jim Deegan, from *Hotter Than a Bandit's Shotgun and Other Stories* (Canmore: Coyote Books, 1996). Excerpted from *Hotter Than a Bandit's Shotgun and Other Stories*, with permission of the publisher, Coyote Books.

"A Bear of a Story" from the Banff *Crag and Canyon*, 7 May 1975. Reprinted by permission of the Banff *Crag and Canyon*.

"Incident at Spray Lake" by Dan McCowan, from *Animals of the Canadian Rockies* (New York: Dodd, Mead & Co., 1936).

"The Lonely Struggle of Tom Bedell" by Lukin Johnston, from *Beyond the Rockies* (London: J.M. Dent & Sons, 1929).

"The Death of a Warden" by Howard O'Hagan, in "Death Lurks in Silence," from *The* [Victoria] *Daily Colonist*, 23 December 1962. Reprinted by permission of the Victoria *Times Colonist*.

"At Grips with a Grizzly" by Colin Wyatt, from *In Jeopardy*, Theresa M. Ford, ed. (Edmonton: Alberta Education, 1979). Reprinted by permission of Maclean's Magazine, from the issue of 15 March 1953.

"Hit-and-Run" by Harry Rowed, in "To Each a Grizzly," from *Fifty Years of Trails and Tales*, Marian Goldstream, ed. (Calgary: Skyline Hikers of the Canadian Rockies, 1982). This article is reprinted by kind permission of the Skyline Hikers of the Canadian Rockies, from their book *Fifty Years of Trails and Tales*. The article was written by Harry Rowed, a long-time member of Skyline Hikers.